Boost Your Brain with
Wasabi Wellness

Wasabi for a Healthy Brain

Wasabi for a Healthy Brain

The Japanese Edition Published in 2023 by SHUFUNOTOMO Co., Ltd.

ISBN: 978-1-64273-561-1

Printed in USA
1 2 3 4 5 6 7 8 9 10

Foreword

Before joining a wasabi company, I had never given much thought to wasabi. That changed when I was assigned to the research division and encountered Real wasabi—native Japanese wasabi—for the first time. I took home some leftover wasabi from a lab test and decided to try it with soba noodles. The soba itself was nothing special, just standard dried noodles from the supermarket. At work, I learned the proper way to enjoy wasabi: place freshly grated wasabi directly onto the noodles, and be sure not to let it soak in the *mentsuyu* dipping sauce.

As I took a bite, the refreshing green aroma of Real wasabi wafted gently through my nose, while the flavors of the soba and the *mentsuyu* unfolded in my mouth in three delicious layers. The rich and nuanced flavors felt like a revelation. That was the moment I truly awakened to the taste of Real wasabi. I also found myself wondering what kind of wasabi I had been eating all these years.

As I began researching Real wasabi, which was historically used as a medicinal herb, I was further amazed by its potent health effects. While many ingredients show promise in preliminary studies, it is rare to see such clear results in real-world applications. The impact of Real wasabi on the brain, especially its potential to support cognitive function, will only become more significant as we enter the era of 100-year lifespans.

Unfortunately, the wasabi sold in shelf stable tubes at supermarkets contains only minute amounts of the grated rhizome that defines true Real wasabi. These products, prioritizing convenience, offer minimal nutritional value and resemble little more than spicy green paste.

Native to Japan, Real wasabi is a precious plant, prized not only for its vibrant flavor but also for its health benefits. And yet, products bearing little resemblance to the real thing have proliferated. Domestic cultivation of Real wasabi, which stood at 5,000 tons in 2000, had declined to less than 2,000 tons by 2020—and the trend continues downward.

In recent years, there has been more research into the functional properties of wasabi, and products like wasabi supplements have begun to appear on the market. However, it is important to note that wasabi's key active compound, hexaraphane, is difficult to extract and process. Some products may not contain sufficient amounts of the effective ingredient.

As a specialist in wasabi research, I hope to raise awareness of these realities, encourage more people to savor the flavor of genuine wasabi, and explore its potential health benefits. It is with this intention that I have written this book.

Isao Okunishi, Ph.D. (Agricultural Science)
Kinjirushi Co., Ltd.

Contents

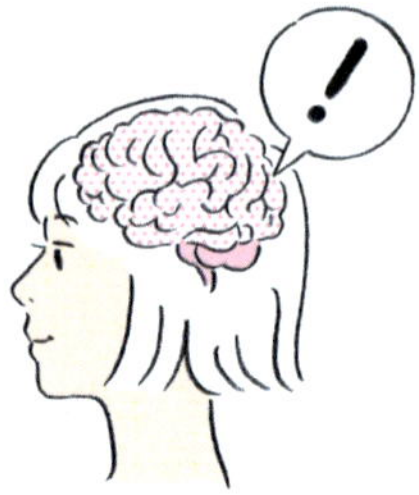

Part 1

Keep the Brain Healthy with Wasabi

Part 2

Time to Start Your Wasabi Wellness Routine

Want to Know More about Wasabi?

Part 3

Part 1

Brain Detox

Keep the Brain Healthy with Wasabi

Hexaraphane, a compound found in Real wasabi has powerful antioxidant properties that help protect cells from damage, keeping the brain active and healthy. We spoke with an expert who has been studying the potential health benefits of wasabi.

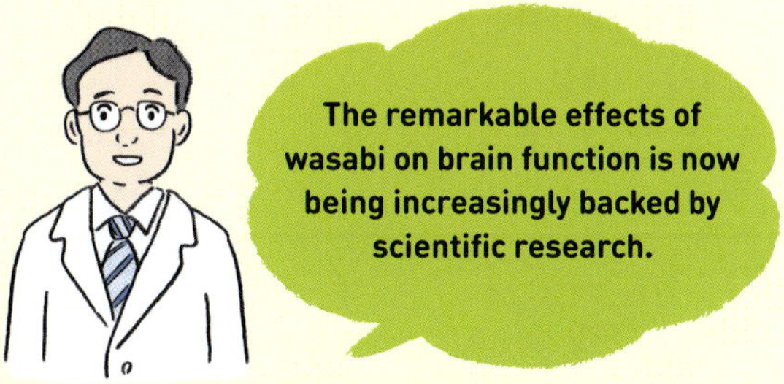

Interview with Dr. Rui Nouchi

What Makes a Brain "Healthy"?

Q: What are the differences between a healthy brain and one that isn't functioning well?

Dr. Nouchi: The differences are actually quite striking. If we look at brain volume, for example, individuals with cognitive decline—such as those with dementia—tend to have significantly smaller brain volumes compared to healthy individuals. The most pronounced atrophy is often seen in the hippocampus, a region critical for memory, and this shrinkage can also extend to the frontal lobe and prefrontal cortex.

It's not easy to define exactly what constitutes a "healthy" brain, but we know that people who demonstrate effective cognitive performance typically show high levels of brain activity. In particular, the dorsolateral prefrontal cortex (DLPFC)—part of the frontal lobe—is more active in such individuals. When this area of the brain is functioning well, people are better able to tackle complex tasks and challenges.

So, we could say that a "healthy brain" is one that has not undergone significant shrinkage and shows appropriate, dynamic activity in key areas.

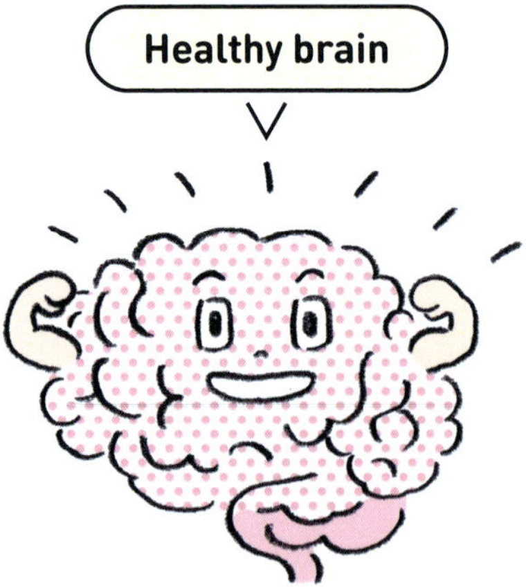

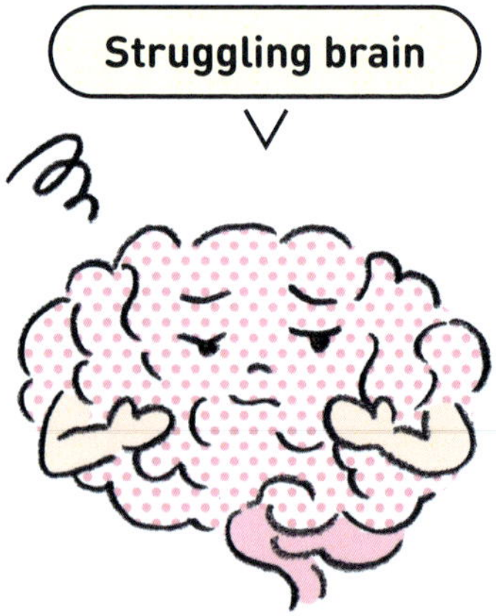

Struggling brains have a shrunken prefrontal cortex and hippocampus.

Brain structure

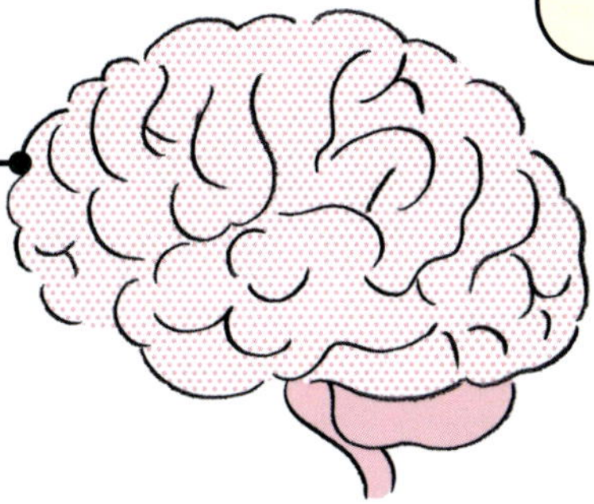

Q: What roles do the hippocampus and frontal lobes play in the brain?

Dr. Nouchi: The hippocampus is primarily responsible for memory, especially long-term memory and what we call episodic memory, such as remembering someone's name, recalling past events, or imagining future scenarios. In short, it's a critical region for the kinds of memory we rely on in daily life. The prefrontal cortex, on the other hand, governs what are often referred to in textbooks as "higher-order cognitive functions." It's also described as the part of the brain that makes us distinctly human. More specifically, the frontal lobe enables us to practice self-control, make decisions, and follow through.

Q: What are the key factors in maintaining a healthy and active brain?

Dr. Nouchi: There are four essential elements: regular physical exercise, active social engagement, cognitive stimulation, and a balanced, nutritious diet. These pillars form the foundation for supporting brain health and activity.

Dr. Rui Nouchi

Associate Professor at the Institute of Development, Aging, and Cancer, Tohoku University (Distinguished Researcher, Ministry of Education, Culture, Sports, Science and Technology). He specializes in psychology and cognitive health science. In 2020, he received the International Award from the Japanese Psychological Association in recognition of his contributions to the field.
(Currently School of Psychological Sciences, University of Human Environments)

Dr. Rui Nouchi's Guide to a

Healthier Brain

Four key pillars for a healthy brain

To keep your brain functioning at its best, Dr. Nouchi emphasizes the importance of four key factors: exercise, social connection, cognitive stimulation, and nutrition. These aren't just essential for maintaining brain health—they are also deeply connected to the causes of cognitive decline.

"It's difficult to single out which of the four elements has the greatest impact when missing," says Dr. Nouchi. "In reality, each one plays an essential role, and they're all deeply interconnected. For example, exercise can go hand-in-hand with eating nutritiously or help maintain social connections. In other words, these work best when combined in daily life."

Exercising regularly

In simple terms, "exercise" means regular physical activity, "social connections" involves maintaining communication and relationships with others, "cognitive stimulation" refers to engaging the brain through mental challenges like brain-training games, and "nutrition" means maintaining a healthy, balanced diet. Living with these four pillars in mind is, according to Dr. Nouchi, one of the most effective ways to support long-term brain vitality.

WASABI COLUMN

Brain-Boosting Tips

- Aim to exercise for at least 30 minutes, three times a week.
- Stay socially connected—having friends you can rely on and speaking with someone every day makes a difference.
- Engage in cognitive activities like brain-training around three times a week.
- Maintain a nutritious, balanced diet to support both body and mind.

Communicating with others

Healthy meals

The brain doesn't have to decline with age—it has the remarkable ability to regenerate.

"Many people think that the brain and the body peak in early adulthood and then just decline from there," Dr. Nouchi says. "But the brain is actually quite fascinating. In the hippocampus especially, we now know that neurogenesis—the creation of new neurons—continues to occur throughout life. New cells are constantly being generated."

Neurogenesis in the hippocampus isn't limited by age; it happens regularly, even in older adults. Research has repeatedly shown that exercise, particularly aerobic exercise, can enhance this process and even increase the size of the hippocampus. "When the brain is actively creating new neurons, and you support it with exercise, cognitive training, or specific nutrients, it can change its structure, even in old age," Dr. Nouchi explains.

"Intervening through exercise, social connection, cognitive stimulation, and nutrition can significantly boost brain health." he continues. "It's a well-established fact now: even in later life, we can improve the brain."

Regular cognitive training

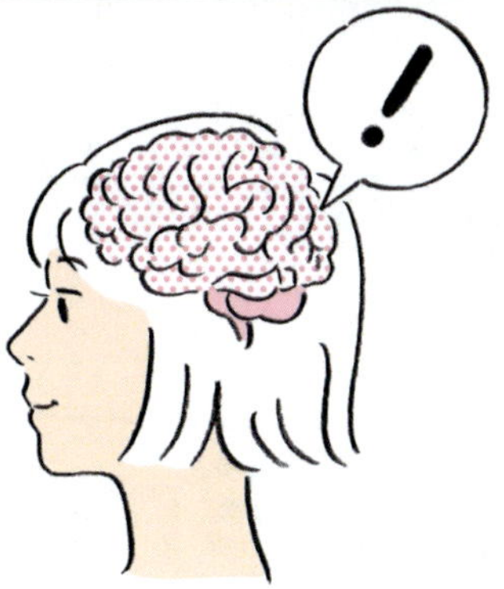

Wasabi's anti-inflammatory and antioxidant properties improve cognitive function!

Nutrition: The most accessible first step

Dr. Nouchi acknowledges that it's not always easy to practice all four elements of a brain-healthy lifestyle, so he recommends starting with the most accessible: nutrition. Unlike the other three, improvements in diet can be implemented with relatively little effort and can complement the rest.

"For someone who doesn't exercise much, asking them to exercise for 30 minutes a day three times a week might feel overwhelming," he says. "But asking them to adjust their diet or incorporate a specific nutrient? That's much easier. Nutritional changes are less intimidating, less tiring, and easier to stick with over time."

Why choose wasabi?

"One of the reasons wasabi supports cognitive health and overall wellness is its powerful anti-inflammatory and antioxidant properties," Dr. Nouchi explains. "These effects

Clear Your Mind with Real wasabi: A Detox for the Brain

Real wasabi excels at activating anti-oxidant enzymes.

aren't unique to wasabi—many plant-based foods offer them. However, the compounds found in wasabi are particularly potent."

"Another advantage of wasabi," Dr. Nouchi explains, "is that as a condiment, it pairs easily with a wide variety of dishes." While many ingredients require large quantities to achieve a beneficial effect, high-quality Real wasabi delivers health-supporting compounds in just a small daily amount: five grams a day. Its ease of use and potential for everyday, long-term incorporation into the diet are key reasons why researchers are increasingly paying attention to this remarkable ingredient.

If any of this sounds familiar, your brain might be ready for a detox!

Lately, I've been so forgetful.

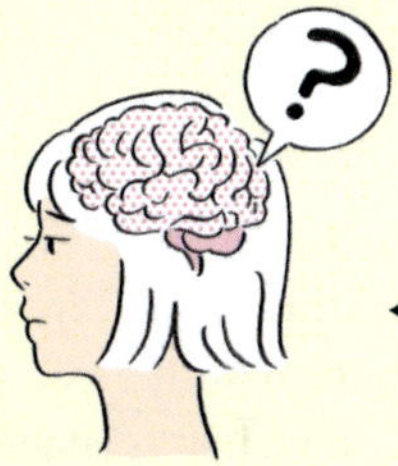

Struggling to recall names or feeling like your memory just isn't what it used to be? Don't chalk it up to aging too quickly—lifestyle changes that support brain health can help turn things around.

I want to prevent dementia.

Shrinkage of the hippocampus and prefrontal cortex is commonly seen in dementia and even in normal aging. The good news? Improving your diet is a great place to start.

Among more than 20 vegetables studied for their detoxifying and antioxidant enzyme-inducing properties, Real wasabi stood out as one of the most effective.

Why Real wasabi is Great for Your Brain

The antioxidant properties of wasabi protect cells from damage

Research from both basic and animal studies has revealed the remarkable antioxidant properties of Real wasabi. This is thanks to a compound found in the rhizome called hexaraphane (6-MSITC). While well-known antioxidants like vitamin C and polyphenols work by neutralizing reactive oxygen species after they form in a "scavenger-type" mechanism, hexaraphane is different; it actually prevents the formation of reactive oxygen species (ROS) in the first place in an "inhibitory-type" antioxidant mechanism. What's more, hexaraphane's effects last for 24 hours after a single dose, helping to maintain cellular health over time, not just in the brain but throughout the entire body.

Unlike other cells in the body, neurons (nerve cells) are difficult to regenerate once damaged. This is why preventing oxidative stress in the first place is critical. While vitamin C and polyphenols can help if damage occurs, it's hexaraphane that supports long-term brain health by protecting neurons before harm is done. By reducing the chance of oxidative damage, wasabi becomes a powerful ally in maintaining your brain's overall quality and performance.

Hexaraphane prevents the generation of harmful reactive oxygen species!

Hexaraphane: A Powerful Compound in Real wasabi

Think of oxidative stress like a fire. Polyphenols act like firefighters—rushing in after the fire starts. Hexaraphane, on the other hand, works like a shut-off valve that prevents the fire from starting in the first place.

What Is Hexaraphane?

A bioactive compound found in the rhizome and roots of Real wasabi, hexaraphane works by suppressing the generation of ROS, helping to prevent damage to brain cells. Its effects are long-lasting—up to 24 hours after a single dose.

Active compound

Hexaraphane
(6-MSITC)

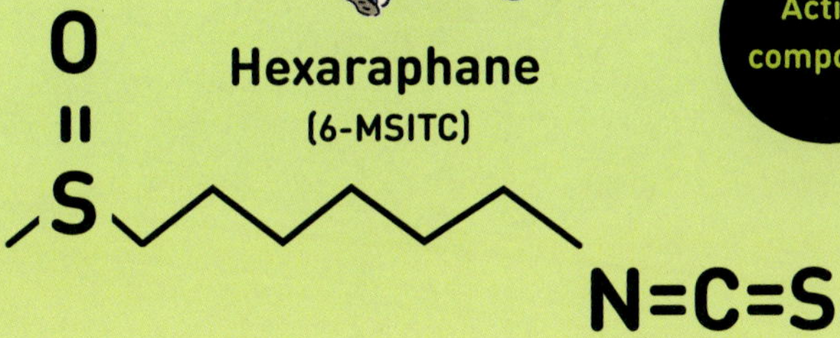

Properties

Antioxidant properties
Cognitive function support

Hexaraphane has been shown to have a wide range of potential benefits:

Hexaraphane offers a wide range of benefits, including antioxidant effects, support for cognitive function, induction of detoxifying enzymes, suppression of cancer metastasis, and even promotion of hair growth. By activating antioxidant enzymes, it enhances the body's overall defense against oxidative stress, and its effects last for up to 24 hours, making it ideal for intake once a day.

Hexaraphane retains its effect for 24 hours. According to the criteria for functional food labeling in Japan, the effective daily intake of hexaraphane is 0.8 mg—about one teaspoon of Real wasabi.

Real wasabi's Antioxidant Properties Rank Top-level among Vegetables and Fruits!

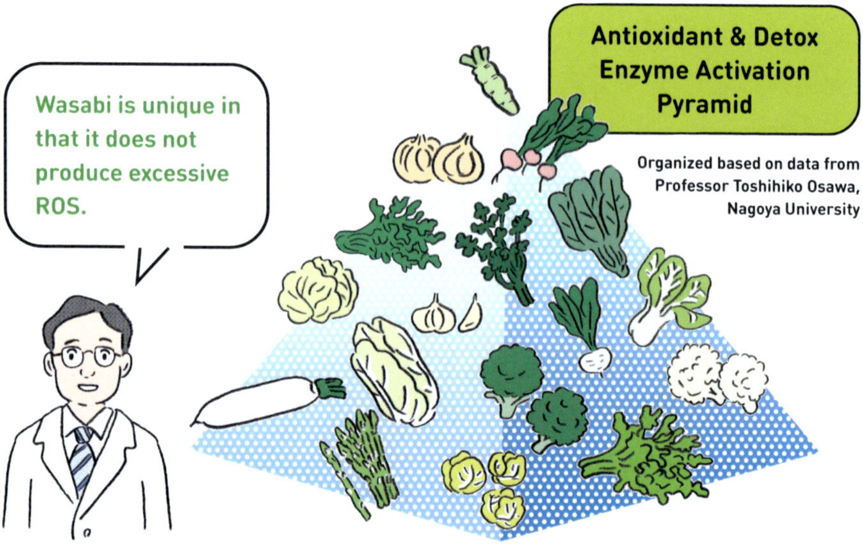

Real wasabi's antioxidant properties are now in the spotlight

Until recently, antioxidant capabilities were typically measured by inducing ROS and observing how well other substances could counteract the resulting oxidation. However, this method cannot detect the preventive effects of Real wasabi, which works by suppressing the generation of ROS in the first place. As a result, Real wasabi's potent antioxidant properties went largely unrecognized.

It is only recently that the remarkable antioxidant effects of Real wasabi have begun to attract attention, and they are now understood to be top-level among vegetables and fruits.

Another fascinating finding about Real wasabi has also emerged. In Japan, there is a long-standing culinary tradition of eating wasabi with sushi and sashimi. Now, scientific research suggests that combining Real wasabi with fish has synergistic benefits.

In cell-based studies, the combination of hexaraphane and the DHA

Synergistic Benefits When Combined with DHA from Fish

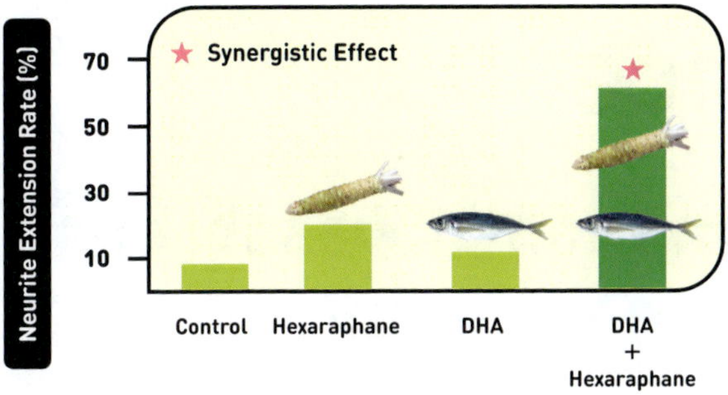

The Combined Power of Hexaraphane and DHA

In a cell study where neural cells were cultured for 72 hours in the presence of nerve growth factor, both the growth of neurites and the production of dopamine, were measured. The results showed a clear synergistic effect when hexaraphane combined with DHA.

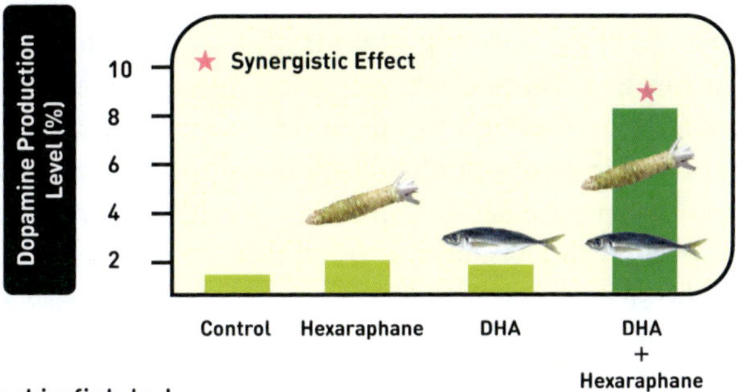

(omega-3 fatty acid) found in fish led to greater extension of dendrites—branches of nerve cells—as well as increased production of dopamine, a key neurotransmitter. These effects were significantly more pronounced than when each component was administered on its own. This strongly indicates that the traditional pairing of fish and Real wasabi may offer real cognitive benefits, showing that the wisdom of Japanese culinary heritage is backed by modern science.

WASABI COLUMN

Sushi and wasabi: A pairing that makes sense from a health perspective

Until now, adding wasabi to sushi or sashimi has mainly been appreciated for its culinary benefits—specifically, how it masks the fishy odor. However, the recent discovery of the synergistic effects between DHA and hexaraphane has revealed that this traditional pairing isn't just delicious, but also makes perfect sense from a health perspective.

The Power of Wasabi, Now Backed by Science

Daily consumption of wasabi shown to improve cognitive function

Growing scientific evidence for wasabi's brain-boosting benefits

The positive effects of wasabi on the brain are increasingly being backed by scientific studies. Let us start with an experiment using mice.

Amyloid beta is a type of protein produced in the brain, and its accumulation is a known characteristic of Alzheimer's disease. In one study, researchers used genetically modified mice that produce large amounts of amyloid beta. These mice exhibit symptoms similar to those of humans with Alzheimer's, such as sluggish movement and memory decline. When these mice underwent memory tests, their performance was worse than that of healthy mice. However, when given hexaraphane, the functional compound found in Real wasabi, their decline was significantly slowed.

Another protein closely associated with the development of Alzheimer's is tau. When tau undergoes a process called phosphorylation, it can damage brain cells and accelerate cognitive decline. Research has shown that hexaraphane may also help inhibit this phosphorylation process, suggesting its potential role in preventing the onset of Alzheimer's.

But do these effects extend to humans? One study set out to find out, as shown in the graph on page 19. The participants were older adults who generally did little exercise. A total of 37 individuals between the ages of 45 to 68 were divided into two groups: one group received 100 mg of Wasabi-sulfinyl™ (a Real wasabi-derived supplement rich in hexaraphane), while the other received a placebo. Both groups then took the same test—a Stroop task. In the Stroop task, participants are

Regular Wasabi Intake Supports Cognitive Function

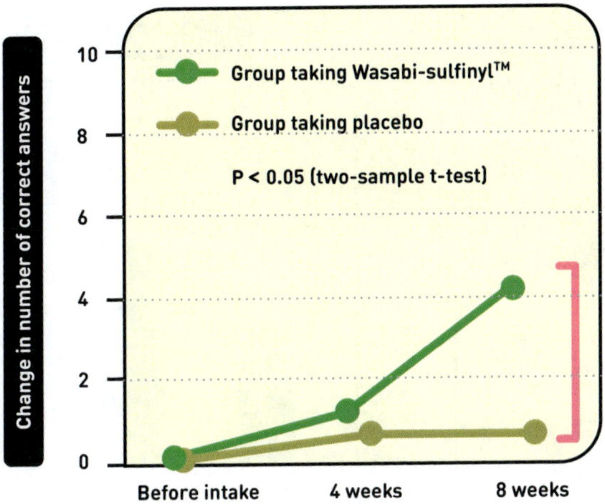

*Placebo: a dummy supplement without Wasabi-sulfinyl™.

What Is Wasabi-sulfinyl™?

Wasabi-sulfinyl™ is a food ingredient made by extracting and concentrating hexaraphane from the roots and rhizomes of Real wasabi. It allows you to easily incorporate this powerful compound into your daily routine.

Cognitive function tested through the Stroop task

The Stroop task is a test used to evaluate cognitive function. Results clearly show that the group taking Wasabi-sulfinyl™ achieved higher accuracy scores at both the 4-week and 8-week marks.

asked to say the color of the font a word is written in, rather than the word itself. For example, if the word "red" is written in green, the correct answer is "green." This task is widely used to assess cognitive function. The results showed that the group who took Wasabi-sulfinyl™ had a higher accuracy rate after both four and eight weeks, clearly demonstrating improved cognitive performance.

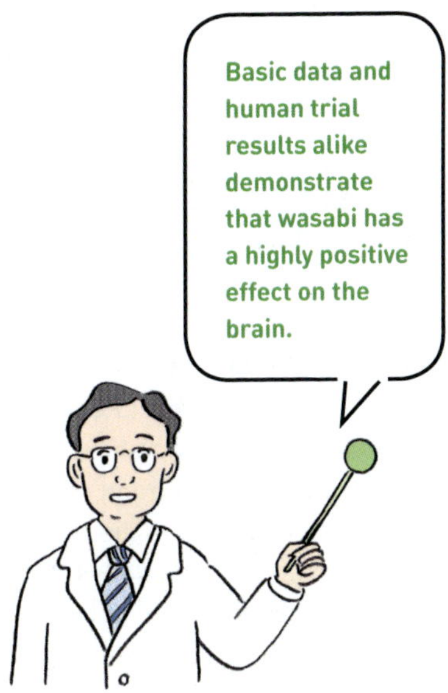

Wasabi Can Make Your Brain Younger!

Wasabi has been shown to boost attention and decision-making skills!

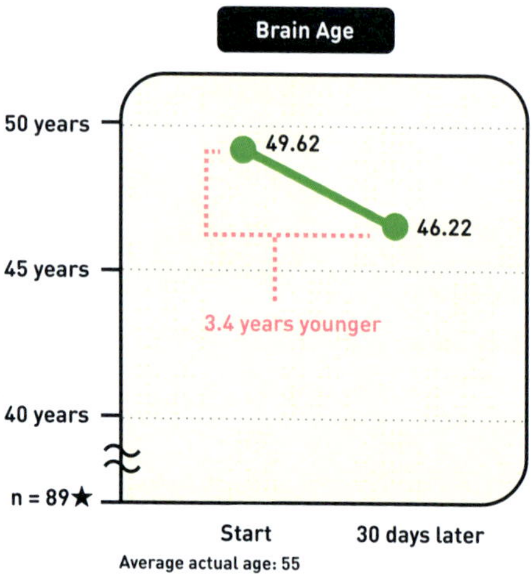

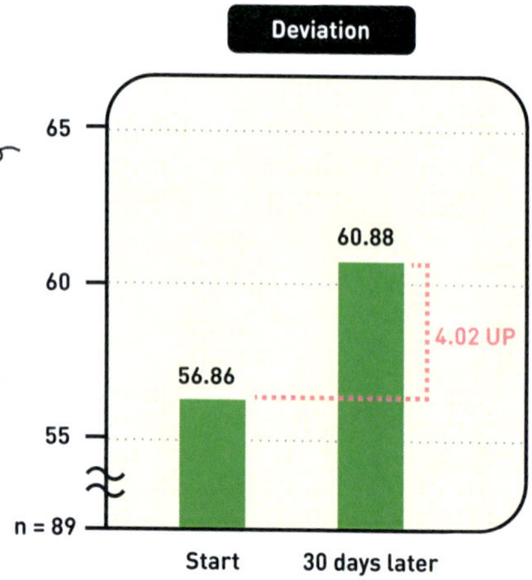

Wasabi-sulfinyl™ 200 mg/day intake (Nomon Co., Ltd.)

One 100 mg dose of Wasabi-sulfinyl™ contains 0.8 mg of hexaraphane.

One month of wasabi intake improves brain age and cognitive scores

Another clinical study has also revealed the benefits of Real wasabi. The two graphs above show changes in brain age and deviation scores based on results from the Brain Assessment, a cognitive test by the Research Institute of Brain Activation. In these types of tests, average scores tend to gradually decline from one's 40s through the 70s, and from the scores, both brain age and deviation scores can be calculated. Naturally, the higher the deviation score and the younger the brain age, the healthier the brain is considered to be. If there is a significant gap between one's actual age and the test score, it suggests signs of brain decline or an increased risk

Take 1–2 Teaspoons of Real wasabi Every Day!

To get the same amount of hexaraphane as found in a supplement (0.8–1.6 mg), you would need about 1–2 teaspoons (5–10 grams) of Real wasabi.

WASABI COLUMN

Since the effect of hexaraphane lasts for 24 hours, daily intake is essential.

Hexaraphane's beneficial effects continue for 24 hours, so it's important to consume it every day. Clinical studies have also shown that continuous intake leads to greater effects at 8 weeks compared to 4 weeks. The key is to maintain daily intake for as long as possible.

of dementia, indicating the need for proactive measures.

The graphs on the left page show the results of a test involving 89 participants who took Wasabi-sulfinyl™ (200 mg/day). After just 30 days, their brain age had rejuvenated by an impressive 3.4 years, and their deviation score had improved by 4.02 points. Achieving a 3.4-year reduction in brain age after simply taking Wasabi-sulfinyl™ daily for a month is a truly remarkable outcome. A variety of clinical studies like these demonstrate the positive effects of Real wasabi.

Consuming Wasabi Helps Improve Memory, Too

In the study, 72 Japanese seniors aged 60 and older were divided into two groups: one group of 36 participants took 100 mg of Wasabi-sulfinyl™ daily over 12 weeks, while the other 36 participants served as a placebo group. Researchers assessed a wide range of cognitive functions and the results were promising. Participants who took Wasabi-sulfinyl™ showed notable improvements in both working memory and episodic memory compared to those in the placebo group.

Working memory refers to the ability to temporarily store and process information. It is essential for tasks such as remembering details during conversations,responding appropriately, and efficiently organizing work. Episodic memory, on the other hand, allows us to recall personal experiences, such as remembering names and faces or retaining information from daily life.

Both types of memory tend to decline naturally with age. An increase in forgetfulness can sometimes signal the beginning of this decline, making interventions that support memory all the more valuable.

In the study, working memory was evaluated through the Digit Span Backward Test (DS-B), where participants were asked to repeat

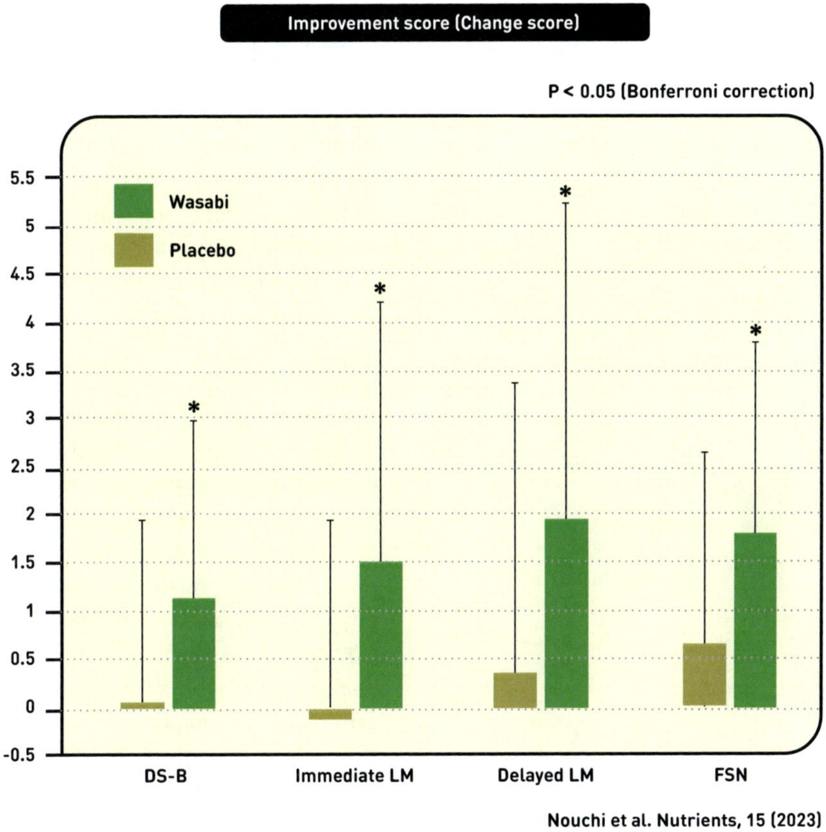

sequences of numbers in reverse order. Episodic memory was assessed using the Logical Memory test, which involved listening to a short story and recalling it immediately (Immediate LM) as well as 30 minutes later (Delayed LM). Another test, known as the Face and Second Name Test (FSN), measured the ability to match faces with corresponding names. Across all assessments, the group taking Wasabi-sulfinyl™ demonstrated statistically significant improvements.

Wasabi Can Help Clear Brain Fog

Brain fog can also arise from chronic fatigue syndrome

Brain fog—a condition marked by sluggish thinking, poor concentration, and mental fatigue—gained widespread attention as a lingering symptom of long COVID-19. According to Prof. Takakazu Oka, this phenomenon has long been recognized as a symptom of cognitive dysfunction in patients with chronic fatigue syndrome (CFS).

"Many people experiencing prolonged symptoms such as generalized fatigue or brain fog after COVID-19 for over six months are beginning to meet the diagnostic criteria for chronic fatigue syndrome," explains Prof. Oka. "A key mechanism common to both conditions is inflammation within the brain."

During COVID-19, much was made of the so-called cytokine

Professor Takakazu Oka

Professor and Chair of Psychosomatic Medicine, School of Medicine, International University of Health and Welfare. His specialties include the treatment of psychogenic fever, chronic fatigue syndrome, orthostatic dysregulation, and functional gastrointestinal disorders storm, a surge of inflammatory cytokines*1 that spreads throughout the body. These cytokines can activate microglial cells in the brain, triggering chronic inflammation. This inflammation, in turn, can impair neurotransmission, reduce cerebral blood flow, and ultimately lead to structural changes in the brain. "We now believe that this kind of chronic neuroinflammation plays a significant role in the development of cognitive symptoms," Oka adds.

Wasabi and Cognitive Recovery

Prof. Oka explains that various studies show that wasabi may be an effective tool in dealing with cognitive dysfunction arising from chronic fatigue syndrome. "Animal studies conducted by Dr. Yosuke Kataoka's group at Riken, the Institute of Physical and Chemical Research, have shown that oral administration of hexaraphane, the compound found in wasabi, improved inflammation in the brain.

Building on this, Prof. Oka conducted a small-scale clinical study involving 15 participants. Each subject was administered a fixed dose of a supplement containing Wasabi-sulfinyl™ (produced by Nomon Inc.) over a set period to observe potential improvements in cognitive and neurological symptoms.*2

The results were compelling. Participants reported noticeable improvements in headache frequency, muscle pain, brain fog, language recall difficulty, and light sensitivity. These findings strongly suggest that hexaraphane's effects target neurocognitive symptoms.

Objective cognitive assessments reinforced the subjective reports. In one such test, participants were asked to draw lines connecting the numbers 1 through 25 in sequence that were randomly distributed on a sheet of paper. Before taking the supplement, participants averaged 53 seconds to complete the task. After supplementation, the average

The following subjective symptoms showed improvement:

- ▶ **Severity of brain fog**
- ▶ **Frequency of headaches**
- ▶ **Frequency of muscle pain**
- ▶ **Difficulty verbalizing thoughts**
- ▶ **Sensitivity to light (photophobia)**

*1 Cytokines are small molecule proteins secreted mainly by immune cells. They play a role in the transmission of information between cells.

*2 Take 1.2g/day of Wasabi-sulfinyl™

Cognitive Function Test
Trail Making Test-A

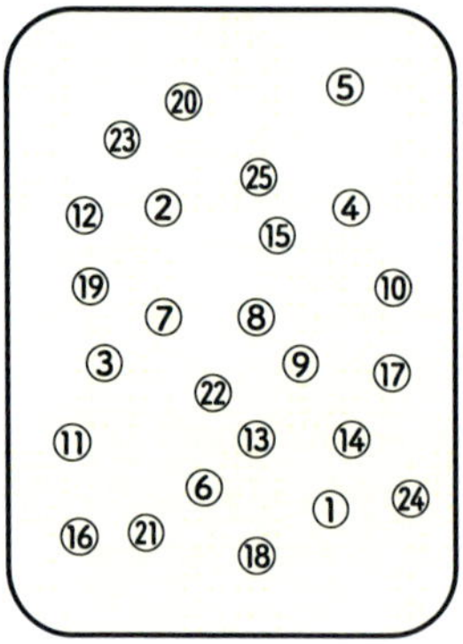

In this cognitive test, participants were asked to trace numbers from 1 to 25 in order on a sheet of paper.

For healthy individuals: Ages 20–30s: 29 ± 8 seconds, 40s: 30 ± 8 seconds
After taking the wasabi supplement, participants showed significant improvement: From 53.0 ± 16.3 seconds to 38.1 ± 13.9 seconds
$(P < 0.01)$

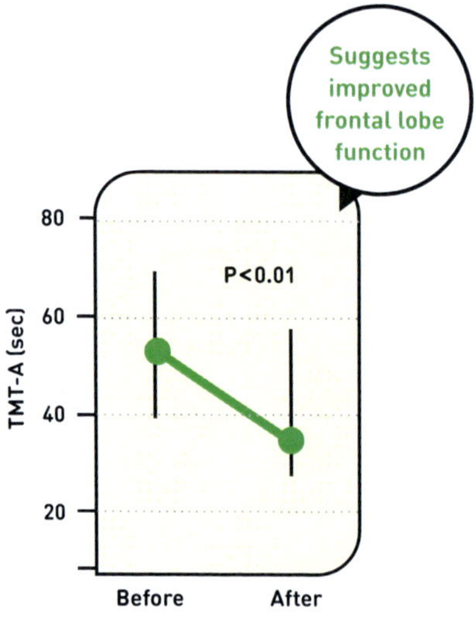

dropped to 38 seconds—a substantial improvement and a likely indicator of enhanced frontal lobe activity.

No Other Ingredient Has Shown This Level of Effectiveness

Following the 12-week study, patients who had taken Wasabi-sulfinyl™ were asked to describe the changes they experienced. The responses revealed significant improvements in cognitive function. One participant wrote, "Before, it always felt like there was a fog in my head, as if part of my brain had shut down and couldn't move—heavy and stuck. But now, I can organize my thoughts."

Another shared, "Words that used to get stuck now come to me more easily, and I can take notes while reading." A third noted, "I used to only be able to concentrate for about ten minutes, but now I can spend nearly an hour reading and summarizing documents."

Reflecting on these results, Prof. Oka shared his optimism about the potential of wasabi: "In treating chronic fatigue syndrome, we've tried vitamins, antioxidants, antidepressants, and a range of traditional herbal remedies. But none of them have shown this level of improvement in cognitive impairment. This is the first time we've seen such an effect."

Note: Chronic fatigue syndrome is now often referred to as myalgic encephalomyelitis/chronic fatigue syndrome (ME/CFS).

Real Stories

The Cognitive Benefits of Wasabi for Chronic Fatigue Syndrome

Case 1: Ms. H (female, 20s)

Initial Symptoms

Before taking wasabi, I suffered from persistent low-grade fever, full-body fatigue, widespread pain (including muscle, joint, and head pain), insomnia, poor appetite, low motivation, and depression. These symptoms left me bedridden for most of the day, leading to muscle loss and a worsening cycle that disrupted my daily life. The fatigue and pain were particularly severe, and the gradual loss of strength made it difficult to find hope for the future. It took a heavy toll on my mental well-being.

After Taking Wasabi

With regular intake of wasabi, I experienced noticeable improvements in my ability to think clearly and in my motivation levels. As a result, my appetite returned, and I once again found joy in eating. This also helped me regain physical strength. Most significantly, the renewed sense of motivation allowed me to take on tasks I previously relied on others for. As I regained independence, my days became more enjoyable, and a sense of hope began to return to my life.

Case 2: Ms. K (female, 20s)

Initial Symptoms

I had a constant mental haze that left me feeling perpetually foggy and unable to think clearly. Planning my day, even simple tasks like cleaning or cooking, required writing things down and carefully considering each step beforehand. I struggled to express myself during conversations, and any focused work would leave me feeling mentally drained within 30 minutes, often triggering headaches or fever. For me, the decline in cognitive function and brain fatigue were the most distressing symptoms.

After Taking Wasabi

I felt a marked improvement after taking wasabi. My head cleared and the heaviness I had felt in my body lifted. I was able to sustain computer work, administrative tasks, and conversations for longer periods without fatigue. In the past, I was consumed by despair at the thought of living with these symptoms indefinitely, but now I experience growing hope with each small improvement, finding emotional relief alongside the physical changes.

\ shelf-stable /

Wasabi in Tubes Has Little to No Effect!

Shelf-stable wasabi paste contains almost no hexaraphane

You might be tempted to run out and buy some wasabi at the supermarket after hearing it can help boost brain function. But unfortunately, most of the commonly available wasabi paste sold in tubes at room temperature contains little to none of the key compound, hexaraphane.

The chart on the right shows hexaraphane content across various wasabi types and products. The highest concentration by far is found in the rhizome—the knobby root portion—of Real wasabi. In contrast, horseradish contains none at all. That's precisely why this book focuses on fresh Real wasabi as the source of this beneficial compound.

The reason most shelf-stable wasabi pastes lack hexaraphane is simple: they are typically made not from the rhizome, but from wasabi stems, horseradish, and other filler ingredients. Only refrigerated or frozen wasabi products, and the rhizome itself were found to retain detectable levels of hexaraphane. In the end, how much rhizome goes into the product makes all the difference.

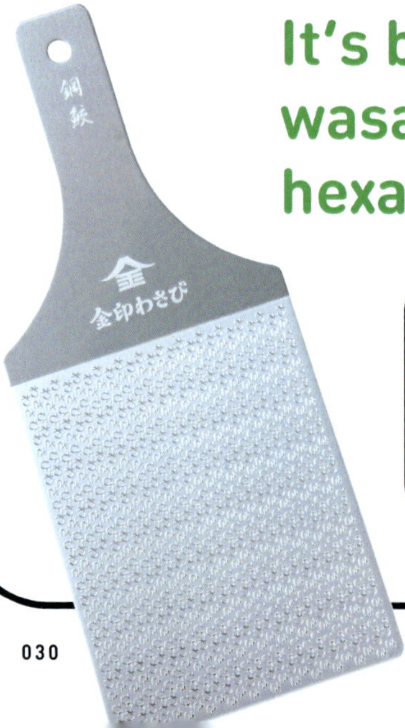

It's best to consume wasabi that contains hexaraphane!

Hexaraphane is only found in Real wasabi!

Hexaraphane content

(Researched by Kinjirushi Co., Ltd.)

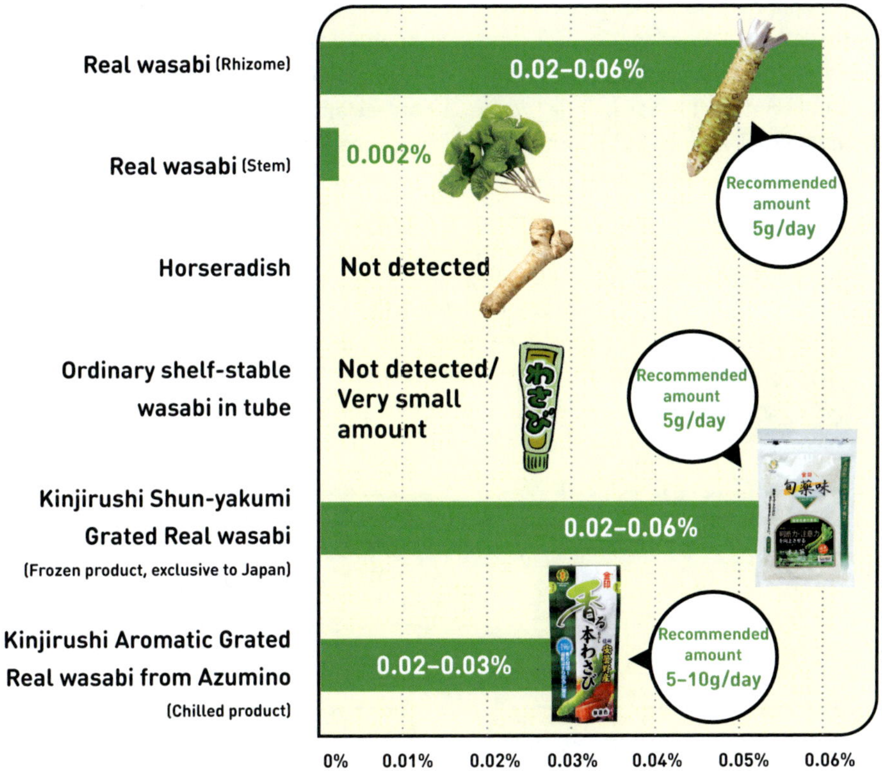

This goes to show that not all wasabi is created equal. If you're going to eat it, why not choose something that's both delicious and good for your health?

More Health Benefits of Real wasabi

Hexaraphane's potential beyond the brain

So far, we've looked at the brain health benefits of hexaraphane found in Real wasabi, but its effects aren't limited to the brain.

One of the biggest threats to our health is oxidative stress, caused by ROS generated through factors like stress and an irregular lifestyle.

These unstable molecules are linked to aging, lifestyle-related

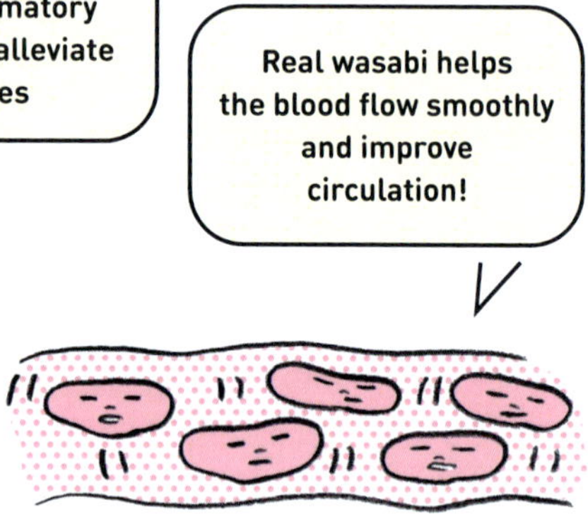

Relief from Allergies

Hexaraphane also shows promise in easing allergy symptoms. In a study involving 16 participants with mild atopic dermatitis, each person took 200 mg of Wasabi-sulfinyl™ daily for two months. A dermatologist assessed their condition and found significant improvements in dry skin and itching, with overall symptom severity reduced.

Blood Flow Smoothly

Real wasabi is among the top vegetables for improving blood flow. In a study where participants consumed 5 grams of Real wasabi, 13 out of 14 people experienced improved blood circulation just one hour later. Better circulation helps reduce the risk of arteriosclerosis, strokes, and heart attacks. It may also be effective in alleviating sensitivity to cold.

illnesses, and a wide range of diseases. Fortunately, hexaraphane helps inhibit the production of these harmful oxidants right at the source, making it an exceptionally potent antioxidant. When people think of antioxidants, they may picture polyphenols or vitamin C, but compared to these, the antioxidant capabilities of Real wasabi is remarkably strong.

The four major health benefits of hexaraphane, as demonstrated by studies, are listed below. But that's just the beginning. Ongoing studies are expected to further uncover the full range of Real wasabi's potential.

Just 5 grams of wasabi a day can support not only brain function, but also broader physical health. Why not make it part of your daily routine?

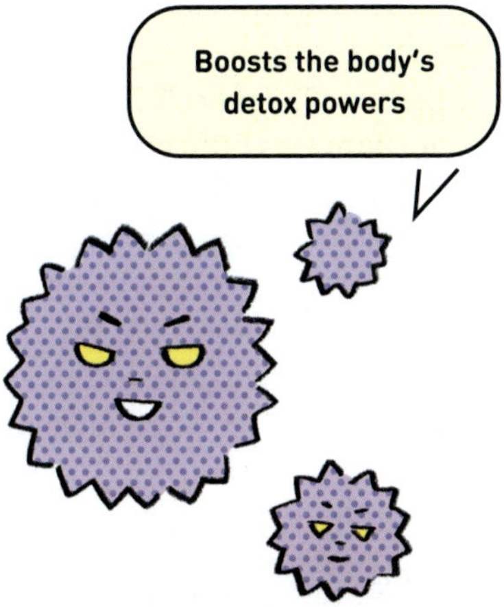

Detoxification & Cancer Prevention

Hexaraphane is one of the most powerful compounds when it comes to activating detoxifying enzymes. These enzymes in the liver play a key role in neutralizing and eliminating toxins from the body. By enhancing this detox function, hexaraphane may also contribute to cancer prevention.

Oxidative Stress Reduction

Wasabi-sulfinyl™also demonstrated the ability to reduce oxidative stress caused by intense physical activity. Participants took Wasabi-sulfinyl™ for 7 days, then performed 30 minutes of aerobic cycling on the final day. The results showed that consuming at least 40 mg daily significantly lowered oxidative stress levels.

The Story Behind the Development of Wasabi-sulfinyl™

Unlocking the unique and powerful potential of hexaraphane

The research that led to the development of Wasabi-sulfinyl™, with hexaraphane as its main active ingredient, began over 20 years ago around the year 2000. Back then, there was little awareness of wasabi's health benefits. A few early studies hinted at anti-cancer properties, but that was about it. Historically, however, wasabi was used as a medicinal herb. This sparked the belief that it must hold

Manufactured into a beneficial food product!

some kind of hidden health potential and became the starting point of a long research journey.

At the time, wasabi was seen strictly as a condiment, and there was almost no research on its chemical components—virtually none.

The early stages of development were far from smooth; it was all about trial and error. Before anything could be commercialized, the first step was confirming safety. Could it be consumed without harm? The main issue was wasabi's pungency, caused by its spicy compounds.

We turned to enzyme reactions for a solution. Wasabi's pungency is created when it's grated—an enzymatic reaction triggers the formation of its sharp flavors. So, we thought, what if we deactivated the enzymes first? We tried heat-treating the wasabi to kill the enzymes, then turning it into powder. Eating it produced no spiciness at all—seemingly a success. But soon after, diarrhea set in for three days. The spicy compounds had still been generated inside the body.

Wasabi-sulfinyl™ powder

That's when we realized we needed to remove the pungent compounds entirely. The challenge? These compounds are chemically similar to the beneficial ones—almost identical in molecular weight—making physical separation difficult.

The breakthrough came from a key difference: the pungent compounds are volatile, while hexaraphane is not. By grating the wasabi and letting the pungency evaporate, they could isolate what remained. That residue, once dried and refined, became the foundation of Wasabi-sulfinyl™, packed with hexaraphane.

Hexaraphane energizes the body's cells!

Even after successfully extracting hexaraphane, we needed to prove it could be absorbed by the human body. So, I did what had to be done: took the compound myself and had my blood drawn for analysis. Back then, testing methods lacked precision, requiring large amounts of blood. At one point, the attending doctor warned, "Any more and this could be dangerous." Despite the risk, we succeeded in detecting hexaraphane in the bloodstream, paving the way for functional studies.

Once research began on the compound's functional properties, we were amazed by the range of effects we discovered. Although we had always believed wasabi contained something good for the body, we hadn't expected such wide-reaching benefits. One of the keys turned out to be hexaraphane's ability to activate Nrf2, a protein present in many types of cells. Nrf2 plays a crucial role in maintaining bodily functions and cellular health. Because it works on a cellular level, its effects are wide-ranging, from improving brain function to boosting overall physical health. When you consider that, the "miraculous" properties of hexaraphane start to seem like a natural result.

Part 2

Practical Application

Time to Start Your Wasabi Wellness Routine

Looking to keep your brain in top shape? Adding Real wasabi to your daily routine can make a real difference. Here are some ideas you can incorporate into your Wasabi Wellness regime.

Real wasabi pairs well with a wide range of dishes. There's no single "right" way to enjoy it—so explore, experiment, and discover your own take on Wasabi Wellness.

Bring Real wasabi into Your Daily Life!

Stay healthy with just one teaspoon of wasabi every day!

In Part 1, we explored the health benefits of Real wasabi. Let's take a moment to review two key points: The effects of hexaraphane—Real wasabi's active compound—last approximately 24 hours, and the recommended daily intake is 5 grams (about 1 teaspoon) of fresh Real wasabi.

Keeping these two facts in mind is the secret to starting your own daily Wasabi Wellness routine. It's not complicated—just one teaspoon a day is all you need. What makes this so appealing is that you don't have to drastically change your lifestyle. By simply adding a small spoonful of Real wasabi to your meals, you can support both your brain and overall health.

Real wasabi is already a familiar ingredient in Japanese cuisine. Its versatility as a condiment is another reason it's so easy to incorporate into your daily diet. Unlike many other health foods, which often require effort and creativity just to reach the recommended daily intake, Real wasabi is easy to add to your everyday meals. It naturally complements a wide variety of dishes, making it one of the most convenient and accessible health foods out there.

Recommended wasabi types		
	Fresh Real wasabi	◎
	Frozen wasabi products	◎
	Refrigerated wasabi product	○
	Shelf-stable wasabi in tubes	×

Easy & Delicious Breakfast Ideas to Start Your Wasabi Wellness Routine

Natto
(Fermented Soybeans)

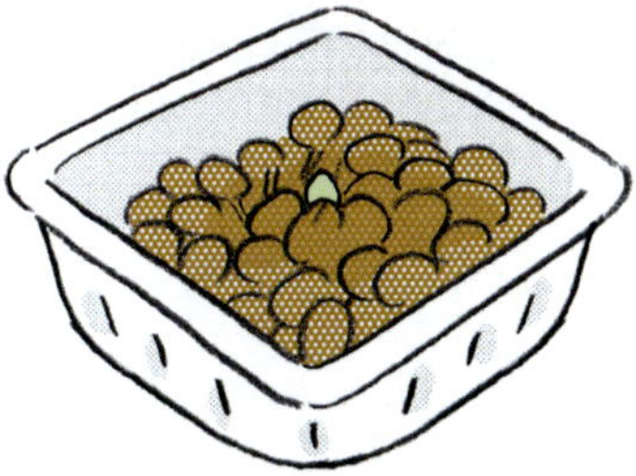

Real wasabi pairs perfectly with natto—another Japanese superfood!

Natto offers a great way to incorporate Real wasabi into your breakfast. Although many eat it with mustard, try swapping it out for Real wasabi instead. It offers the same zesty kick, while wasabi's subtle fragrance enhances the overall taste of the natto.

Cheese Toast

Creamy cheese and spicy wasabi—an unexpectedly great combination!

If you prefer bread in the morning, add a touch of Real wasabi to your cheese toast. While it may sound like an unusual pairing, the rich flavors of cheese balance beautifully with wasabi's sharp kick. One bite might just make it your new favorite!

Tamago-kake Gohan
(Raw Egg Over Rice)

Take this Japanese breakfast classic to the next level with Real wasabi!

This traditional Japanese dish gets a flavor upgrade by turning your usual soy sauce into wasabi soy sauce. Just a small amount transforms your bowl into something new, flavorful, and totally addictive, from the first bite to the last. (Be sure to check if eggs can be consumed raw in your region when preparing this dish.)

Make Lunchtime Wasabi Time with Classic Noodle Dishes

Pasta tends to be a go-to dish for lunch for many people. You can't go wrong by adding wasabi to a soy-sauce based pasta. But that's not the only kind you can pair it with—Real wasabi also enhances creamy pasta dishes thanks to its surprising compatibility with dairy.

Real wasabi pairs wonderfully with soy-based and cream-based pasta dishes

Japanese-Style Pasta

***Kamatama* Udon Noodles**

Swap out ginger for Real wasabi in this beloved udon dish.

Kamatama udon—hot noodles topped with raw egg and soy sauce—is usually served with grated ginger, but try using Real wasabi instead. You'll find it offers an equally delicious kick. Want to go further? Add a dab of butter for an extra layer of flavor. (Be sure to check if eggs can be consumed raw in your region when preparing this dish.)

Boost Your Evening Wasabi Routine with DHA-Rich Fish

Sashimi

Real wasabi is essential for fresh sashimi

Wasabi's traditional use with raw fish isn't just about taste—it also has antibacterial properties and eliminates odor. For proper sashimi etiquette, place a little wasabi directly on the fish rather than mixing it into the soy sauce. The same goes for sushi—it elevates both flavor and safety.

Not just for raw fish—Real wasabi is amazing with rich, grilled varieties too

Grilled Fish

While most people associate wasabi with sashimi, it's also excellent with grilled fish, especially fatty varieties like Atka mackerel. Try replacing grated daikon radish with a small dab of Real wasabi.

10 Dishes That Shine When You Skip the Usual Condiment

Savor the full power of wasabi!

Here are some more ideas to help incorporate wasabi into your daily routine. These 10 creative suggestions make it easy to swap out your usual condiments for Real wasabi.

There are plenty of condiments and spices in everyday Japanese cooking, such as mustard, *shichimi*, and *sansho* pepper, but when it comes to versatility and compatibility with other ingredients, wasabi stands out from the crowd.

Try replacing mustard with wasabi in your go-to Japanese dishes—you'll be surprised how seamlessly it works. That's because the sharp heat of both mustard and wasabi comes from the same compound: allyl isothiocyanate. So, while swapping mustard for wasabi works well, the reverse doesn't always taste quite right. Why? Because wasabi has more than just heat—it brings a complex, aromatic flavor that mustard can't match.

If you're committing to Wasabi Wellness, you may as well enjoy it to the fullest. That's why we've handpicked 10 dishes where wasabi isn't just a substitute—it's a serious upgrade.

Meat Dishes: Just Replace the Sauce with Wasabi for a Gourmet Twist!

Wasabi's punchy flavor pairs wonderfully with grilled meat, giving your dish a more refined finish. Bonus tip: the fat from the meat softens wasabi's sharpness, so don't be shy—use generously. Wasabi soy sauce also works great with steak!

Level up your *yakiniku* with wasabi soy sauce instead of traditional dipping sauce.

Yakiniku
(Grilled Meat)

Shabu-shabu
(Hot Pot)

Skip the chili oil—add wasabi to sesame sauce for an aromatic kick.

Wasabi doesn't just pair well with beef; it's also perfect for pork. Add a dollop to your sesame dipping sauce instead of chili oil. The result is a bold yet balanced flavor that enhances the richness of the meat.

Swap Mustard for Wasabi

Wasabi stimulates the appetite—perfect for hot summer days.

Many people add mustard to chilled ramen salad, but wasabi works just as well. Its natural appetite-boosting effects are ideal for when the summer heat makes eating a chore.

Chilled Ramen Salad

Replace mustard with wasabi for a flavor upgrade.

Dumplings with mustard is a classic, but try swapping in wasabi instead. You'll get the same bold kick, plus a fresh aroma that elevates the whole bite. Dip in soy sauce or ponzu sauce—both work beautifully.

Steamed Dumplings

Unexpected Combos that Work

If you love adding heat to your pizza, try wasabi in place of hot sauce. It might sound odd, but the combo of melted cheese and wasabi is unexpectedly perfect. It's a cross-cultural flavor win that breaks all the culinary rules in a good way.

Try replacing mustard with wasabi in your sandwich spread, or mix wasabi with *mayo* for a creamy, spicy blend. It pairs well with ham, cheese, egg, tuna—pretty much anything you can put between two slices of bread.

Replace *Sansho* Pepper and *Shichimi* with Wasabi for More Refined Flavors

An unbeatable pairing: rich eel and fresh wasabi

Grilled Eel

Grilled eel is typically served with *sansho* pepper but try replacing it with Real wasabi. You'll find it enhances the natural flavors of the eel. The harmony between the eel's fatty texture and wasabi's clean heat creates an unforgettable flavor experience. Once you've tried it, you may never go back to *sansho*.

Add wasabi to your rotation of condiments

Yakitori is often enjoyed with *shichimi* spices or yuzu citrus pepper, but wasabi deserves a spot on the lineup. Its sharp kick and fragrant aroma complement the savory flavors of the chicken. Whether your skewers are seasoned with sauce or just salt, wasabi works well with both. Try rotating between *shichimi*, yuzu *kosho* (yuzu chile paste) and wasabi for a fun flavor adventure.

Yakitori
(Grilled Chicken Skewers)

Other Wasabi-Ready Pairings

Swap the ginger for wasabi and enjoy a fragrant twist

Grilled Eggplant

Grilled eggplant topped with bonito flakes and soy sauce is a classic Japanese dish, but instead of the usual ginger, try wasabi. The spiciness balances the juicy eggplant while adding a refreshing aroma. This simple change turns it into a standout side dish that lets the ingredients shine.

Wasabi adds just the right kick to *takoyaki* and *akashiyaki*

Takoyaki octopus balls are usually served with rich sauces, but wasabi makes an excellent alternative, cutting through the heaviness and adding depth. The same goes for *akashiyaki*, which is traditionally dipped in a light dashi broth. A touch of wasabi in the dipping sauce brings a welcome accent you'll quickly crave.

Takoyaki

12 Easy Wasabi Topping Ideas

Make Real wasabi the star of your meal!

Our last batch of ideas is all about simple wasabi toppings. These quick additions let you enjoy the full flavor of fresh Real wasabi with zero prep—just a swipe is all it takes.

One of Real wasabi's greatest strengths is that it doesn't just act as a supporting flavor; it is the flavor. If you've never tried Real wasabi before, start by placing a bit on your fingertip and tasting it on its own. You'll be amazed by its clean heat, delicate aroma, and rich complexity—worlds apart from the typical store-bought paste.

So when you do eat Real wasabi, try letting it take center stage with menus that highlight its unique charm. One of the best ways to do that is to craft a wasabi rice bowl. Just spoon freshly grated Real wasabi over hot white rice. Top with a generous sprinkle of bonito flakes, and finish with a drizzle of soy sauce. That's it. The simplicity allows the wasabi to shine.

Here are some more ideas to help you enjoy the taste of Real wasabi in an easily-accessible way.

Wasabi: A Simple and Classic Topping

This simple yet iconic dish hails from Izu, one of Japan's top wasabi-producing regions. Just spoon freshly grated Real wasabi over hot white rice topped with a generous sprinkle of bonito flakes, and finish with a drizzle of soy sauce.

The ultimate way to appreciate Real wasabi

Wasabi Rice Bowl

Wasabi-topped crackers: great for parties or snacks

Crackers

Crackers are a blank canvas for all kinds of toppings, so why not wasabi? A dab of Real wasabi makes a bold, elegant snack that's perfect with drinks or at parties. Try it alone or paired with a slice of cheese—it's a match made in *umami* heaven.

Perfect with Dairy! Wasabi Adds a Sharp Kick

Vanilla Ice Cream

Rich vanilla meets a fiery twist of wasabi

Wasabi ice cream and soft serve are beloved local specialties in places like Shizuoka Prefecture. The combination might surprise you, but one bite and you'll be hooked. The richness of vanilla and the sharpness of freshly grated Real wasabi come together for a sophisticated flavor. It's easy to recreate at home, so why not give it a try?

A delightful pairing for your next drink

Cream Cheese

Top cream cheese with a dab of Real wasabi and discover a new favorite snack. This unexpected combo highlights how well wasabi pairs with dairy. Add a pinch of salt or some finely chopped *iburigakko* (smoked and pickled daikon radish) for an even more flavorful experience. It's the perfect companion to your favorite beverage.

White Stew

Elevate your creamy stew with a touch of wasabi

Wondering if wasabi goes with white stew? The answer is a resounding yes. A spoonful of Real wasabi adds a zesty contrast to the stew's mellow richness, bringing out the depth of the flavor without overpowering it.

Add Wasabi for an Instant Salad Upgrade

Transform your usual potato salad with a spoonful of Real wasabi. The spicy kick and aromatic flair add a new dimension, making it a mouthwatering side that goes great with beer. Tuna salad also benefits from the addition—another easy and delicious variation to try.

The perfect beer snack:
wasabi potato salad

Potato Salad

Sesame Dressing

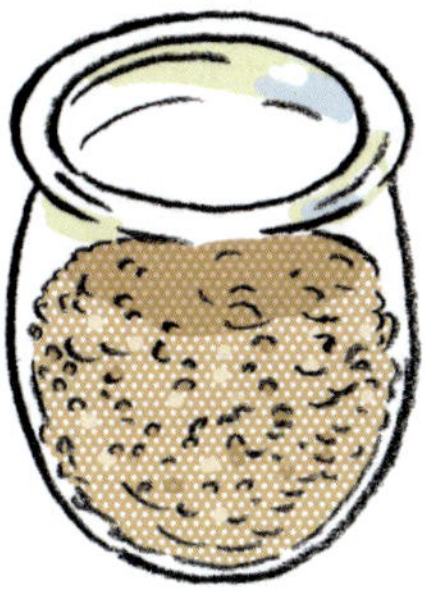

Just a little wasabi makes
sesame dressing pop

Mix Real wasabi into your sesame dressing for a spicy twist that elevates your salad. Wasabi pairs beautifully with creamy or nutty flavors, and this small addition delivers a refined balance of richness and heat.

Tofu Dishes with a Wasabi Twist

Agedashi Tofu

Addictive flavor with wasabi-topped *agedashi* tofu

Wasabi doesn't just go well with dairy; it pairs excellently with tofu. *Agedashi* tofu—deep-fried tofu in broth—is a classic Japanese dish beloved for its silky texture and crispy skin. Add a touch of Real wasabi to enhance the textures and bring out a uniquely bold flavor. It's great as a side dish, or even better with sake.

Tofu Steak

Tofu steak with wasabi soy sauce is a must-try

Tofu steak is a healthy, satisfying alternative to meat, and it pairs perfectly with wasabi soy sauce. For extra depth, try serving it *ankake*-style with a thickened sauce made with potato starch.

Hiyayakko (Chilled Tofu)

Simple yet sublime—wasabi and chilled tofu

One of the best ways to enjoy Real wasabi is with chilled tofu. The clean flavors of tofu let the wasabi's aroma and depth really shine. Top it with bonito flakes or shredded nori seaweed, or try a pinch of salt instead of soy sauce for a subtle, savory finish.

Meat Meets Its Match—Wasabi Completes the Flavor

Tonkatsu is often served with sauce, but try it with salt and Real wasabi instead. The spicy punch of wasabi complements the subtle sweetness of pork, for a deeply satisfying bite. Wasabi soy sauce is another great option.

Bring out the sweetness of pork with wasabi

Tonkatsu **(Pork Cutlet)**

Juicy hamburger steak with wasabi—an unbeatable combo

Hamburger Steak

A juicy patty and freshly grated Real wasabi make for a surprisingly harmonious duo. The wasabi balances the richness of the meat while adding a bright, zesty lift. Whether you go with wasabi soy sauce or wasabi ponzu, it's a guaranteed hit. For something extra, try topping it with avocado.

Wasabi in America: Surprising Pairings That Just Work

Wasabi has a bold, flavorful accent that brings out the best in all kinds of foods, even in Western cooking. Its sharp kick and aromatic freshness cut through rich or greasy dishes, adding a clean, complex layer of flavor. In fact, the more you add, the better it becomes—don't be shy with it!

Just mix a bit of fresh wasabi into mayonnaise and slather it generously over the patty. The wasabi lifts the flavor of the meat, creating a sharper, cleaner bite.

Steak with Japanese-style sauce and wasabi

Though often paired with fish, wasabi is also a fantastic match for meat. Add a dollop of wasabi to steak with soy-based Japanese sauces—or even just salt and pepper—to draw out the beef's natural *umami*.

Teriyaki sauce with wasabi

Hailing from Japan, teriyaki is already a global favorite—but add wasabi, and it reaches new heights. Wasabi complements the sweet-savory sauce perfectly. Drizzle it on chicken or meat. Just be sure to add it fresh, as cooking will mellow out its punch.

Guacamole

Rough-mashed avocado with wasabi, cilantro, onions, lime, and tomato, seasoned with salt and garlic. This spicy twist on classic guacamole is perfect with tortilla chips or crackers and keeps your appetite going.

Add wasabi to the citrus-marinated mix of white fish, tuna, or shrimp with red onion, tomato, lime, cilantro, garlic, and salt. It makes this refreshing summer dish even more invigorating and addictive.

Ceviche

Ham and cheese crackers with wasabi

Hot dog with wasabi *mayo*

Top a cracker with cheese and prosciutto or cured ham, then finish with a touch of wasabi. The salty richness of the meat and cheese is beautifully balanced by wasabi's clean heat. It's perfect with a glass of wine.

Mix wasabi with mayonnaise and slather it over your hot dog. Add chopped veggies, tuna, or cheese for a fun twist. The result? A fresh, sharp take on a familiar favorite.

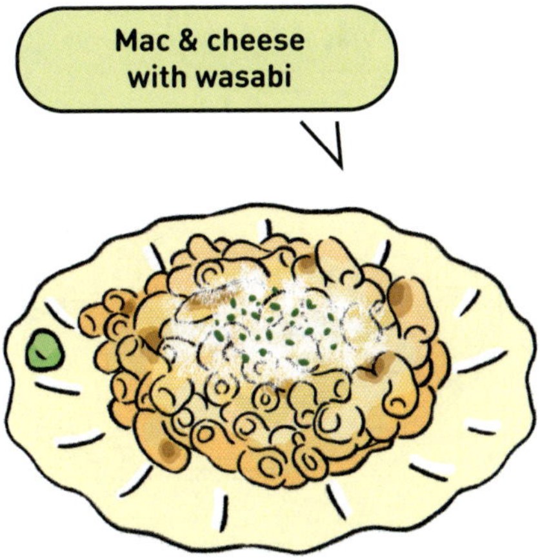

Cheese and wasabi pair beautifully. Add wasabi to piping-hot mac and cheese just before eating. The wasabi's freshness and heat amplify the cheese's depth.

Wasabi and salmon are a natural pair. The smokiness and richness of the salmon is elevated by wasabi's aromatic kick. Enjoy it carpaccio-style or with a few drops of soy sauce.

Seafood and wasabi? Always a win. Top buttery grilled lobster with a generous amount of wasabi. The flavors of the lobster and the richness of the butter are enhanced by wasabi's sharp brightness.

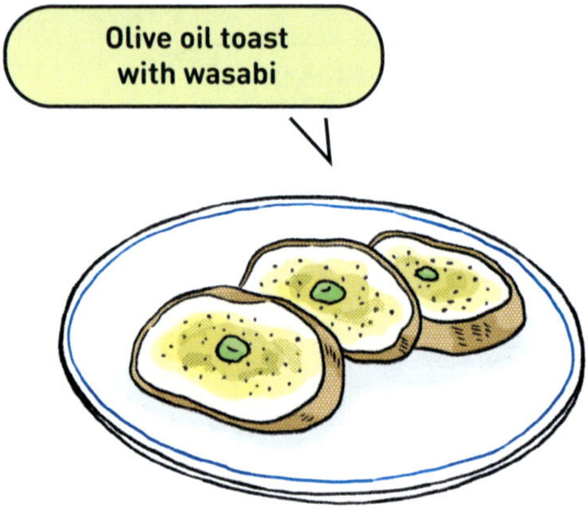

Top crispy white fish with a generous layer of wasabi *mayo*. Since the oiliness can dull the spice, don't be afraid to use wasabi generously. Try it mixed into tartar sauce for a new twist.

Drizzle olive oil over toasted bread, sprinkle with a pinch of salt, and top with wasabi. It's a quick, healthy breakfast that packs a punch. Add sliced tomato or avocado for extra flavor and nutrition.

Mix wasabi into cream cheese and dip your pretzels. It's a surprising combination that makes for a satisfying breakfast or snack—and a delicious way to get your wasabi fix.

Wasabi-based sauces & dressings

Sauces

- Blend puréed avocado, lemon juice, cream, wasabi, soy sauce, grapeseed oil, salt, and pepper. This sauce pairs well with sautéed scallops.
- Mix ponzu, acacia honey, wasabi, and olive oil. Try it on burgers!

Dressings

- Combine grapeseed oil, lemon juice, soy sauce, wasabi, and white pepper. Perfect for salads with persimmon or mango and prosciutto.
- Mix sesame oil, soy sauce, wasabi, lemon juice, and black pepper. Ideal for avocado and salmon salads.

Tuna gratin with wasabi

Wasabi brings out the best in creamy baked dishes, especially ones with tuna or bacon. It enhances the creamy flavor and elevates the toppings. Top your hot gratin with wasabi just before eating to preserve its flavor.

Clam chowder with wasabi

Wasabi is a natural match for creamy seafood soups. Don't cook it in as it will lose its zest. Instead, add it right before serving. It enhances the creaminess and seafood flavors while leaving a refreshing, spicy finish.

No Grating Needed: Frozen & Chilled Wasabi for Easy Everyday Use

In this book, we've been recommending incorporating Real wasabi into your daily routine—a habit we like to call Wasabi Wellness. That's because the key health-boosting compound hexaraphane, which supports brain function, is barely present in most room-temperature tube wasabi products.

When it comes to flavor, true Japanese wasabi culture shines through only when you use fresh Real wasabi. Of course, grating fresh wasabi root can be a lux-

Refrigerated

Frozen and refrigerated wasabi products can offer health benefits!

Kinjirushi Aromatic Grated Real wasabi from Azumino (23 g)

A refrigerated tube made exclusively with flavorful Real wasabi from Shinshu Azumino. Use it just like a regular wasabi tube.

You can expect health benefits from products that are packed with Real wasabi!

urious and mindful experience, but when you're pressed for time, there's a more convenient solution: frozen and refrigerated wasabi products.

Frozen wasabi options offer the rich, authentic taste of fresh Real wasabi with minimal additives. Refrigerated versions may have a slightly milder aroma but are ready to use without defrosting. Importantly, both types contain hexaraphane, unlike most standard wasabi tubes.

As mentioned on page 29, some frozen varieties contain hexaraphane levels comparable to fresh wasabi. Even some refrigerated versions retain about half that amount—more than enough to support your health while enhancing your meals. These frozen and chilled products make it easy to keep up your Wasabi Wellness routine.

Exclusive to Japan

Kinjirushi Frozen Grated Real wasabi
(2 g × 10 packs)

Made with 100% Japanese wasabi and frozen using a specialized method to preserve the natural fragrance and sharpness of fresh wasabi.

Frozen

Kinjirushi Shun-yakumi Grated Real wasabi
(5 g × 20 packs, Online Exclusive)

Grated using a proprietary ultra-low-temperature method to lock in the wasabi's natural aroma and heat at its peak. Comes in convenient single-use sachets.

Frozen

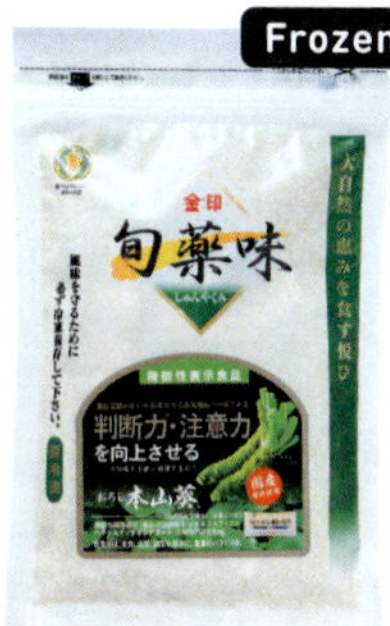

Kinjirushi Aromatic Grated Real wasabi
(20 g, Food with Function Claims)

A refrigerated tube with added hexaraphane, packed with the rich taste and aroma of freshly grated wasabi that enhances the flavors of various ingredients.

Refrigerated

Available online or at fresh seafood and chilled food sections at Japanese supermarkets.

Let frozen and chilled wasabi products support your daily Wasabi Wellness!

Boost Brain Health with Wasabi in Supplement Form!

In addition to frozen and refrigerated wasabi products that help simplify your Wasabi Wellness routine, there's another easy and effective way to enjoy the health benefits of Real wasabi: supplements. While

supplements don't deliver the distinctive taste of wasabi, they are the most efficient and convenient way to get the key health compound hexaraphane.

Historically, wasabi has been used as a medicinal herb in Japan since the Asuka period (538–710 AD). In that sense, wasabi supplements can be seen as a modern continuation of this ancient practice.

They're also ideal for days when you don't have time to cook with wasabi, or if you simply don't enjoy its spiciness but still want the health benefits.

Look for supplements that contain Wasabi-sulfinyl™, a proprietary extract derived from Real wasabi, which includes a concentrated dose of hexaraphane. These modern supplements support the wellbeing of today's busy lifestyles—and are a great way to keep up your Wasabi Wellness.

What is Wasabi-sulfinyl™?

The extract powder is made from Real wasabi using a special process and contains hexaraphane, know to support attention and judgement in middle-aged and older adults who lack regular physical activities, while also helping to improve memory in the elderly.

Beauty from Wasabi Leaves: Skincare & More

Wasabi isn't just a health food—it's also making waves in the beauty world. In addition to hexaraphane's skin benefits, wasabi leaves contain a rare compound called isosaponarin, which stimulates skin cell activity and boosts collagen production.

By your 40s, collagen production can drop to less than half of what it was in your 20s. Wasabi leaf extract can help restore moisture and firmness to aging skin. Some studies have also shown that wasabi leaf compounds may activate brown fat cells, which play a role in preventing weight gain, and stimulate hair growth signals, supporting scalp health and hair regeneration.

Wasabi Leaf-Infused Skincare Products (exclusive to Japan)

Sunsulfee Biyo Facial Soap (100 g)

A wasabi-powered cleansing soap infused with skin-beautifying ingredients from wasabi leaves, perfect for your daily skincare routine.

Sunsulfee Biyo Emulsion (50 mL)

Formulated with the same active ingredients as the lotion, this gentle moisturizer helps combat fine lines and dryness around the eyes and other delicate areas.

Sunsulfee Biyo Lotion (150 mL)

This refreshing lotion combines wasabi leaf extract with a variety of natural beauty ingredients to plump and hydrate your skin.

Biyo means the essence of beauty.
(Clinically tested for wrinkle reduction from dryness.)

How to Enjoy the True Flavor of Real wasabi

Understand wasabi's volatile nature

To truly enjoy the unique flavor of Real wasabi, it's important to know how to handle it properly. The spicy kick of wasabi comes from volatile compounds that dissipate over time. That signature tingling sensation in your nose? It's thanks to these volatile elements.

But that also means the spiciness fades quickly after grating,

Three steps to enjoy wasabi

How to Choose Good Wasabi

The closer the rings, the stronger the flavor.

Look for wasabi roots with closely spaced horizontal lines (or rings). These indicate richer spiciness and a more robust aroma—perfect if you want to fully savor wasabi's natural punch.

How to Use Wasabi in Cooking

Avoid heat to enjoy the spiciness.

Because wasabi's sharpness fades with time and heat, use freshly grated wasabi just before eating to enjoy its full effect.

How to Store Fresh Wasabi

Wrap in paper towels and refrigerate.

To keep your wasabi fresh, wrap the unused portion in a dry paper towel and store it in the refrigerator. Alternatively, you can grate the whole root and freeze it in small, portion-sized wraps using cling film.

and it disappears even faster when exposed to heat. If you want to experience the full flavor and heat of wasabi, it's best to grate it fresh, right before serving. On the other hand, if you're sensitive to its sharpness, you can gently heat it to mellow the spice. The spiciness fades faster than the aroma, so feel free to adjust it to your taste.

For the best texture and flavor, use a fine-toothed grater designed especially for wasabi, which helps break down the fibrous root thoroughly.

How to Prepare Fresh Real wasabi

1

Cut off the leafy stem at the top of the root. The upper part contains more aroma, while the lower part has stronger heat.

2

Use a knife to roughly shave off the small bumps or knobs on the surface.

3

Scrub the root gently with a brush or a traditional *tawashi*. Don't peel the skin—the spicy compounds are concentrated there!

4

Using a wasabi grater, rub the root in a circular motion without applying too much pressure.

Zaru Soba for Connoisseurs: Savoring the Aroma of Real wasabi

Master the right way to use Real wasabi to savor its true taste and enjoy it even more!

A refined way to enjoy soba that highlights every ingredient

When it comes to dishes that simply wouldn't be complete without wasabi, *zaru* soba tops the list. Few foods pair so naturally with wasabi, and none showcase its character quite the same way. However, many people unknowingly miss out on the full experience by using wasabi the wrong way.

A common mistake is mixing the wasabi directly into the dipping sauce. While that may be acceptable with supermarket wasabi paste, it's a waste when using fragrant, premium Real wasabi.

Dipping the wasabi in sauce pre-

Aromatic Ritual: Enjoy the Fragrance Before the First Bite

1

Grate only as much Real wasabi as you need.

2

Press the freshly grated wasabi into the bottom of a small sake cup. Tap it lightly so it sticks.

3

Turn the cup upside down and rest it on the table. Inside the cup, a natural enzymatic reaction will enhance the spiciness and aroma.

4

Wait 2–3 minutes, then lift the cup. A wave of fresh wasabi fragrance will rise, activating your appetite and signaling the start of a delicious meal.

vents you from enjoying its aroma. True wasabi aficionados enjoy Real wasabi by placing a small dab directly on the soba noodles, not in the dipping sauce. This method lets the aroma and flavor of the wasabi shine through. To take it a step further, try dipping your soba in a bit of salt and wasabi instead of any dipping sauce at all. This minimalist approach brings out the full flavor of the soba and wasabi, making it a sophisticated way to enjoy a classic dish. Master this technique and share the experience with others!

Column

Know Your Real wasabi: Cooking Tips to Match Your Taste

Real wasabi pairs well with a wide variety of dishes and ingredients, so why not try creating your own original recipes? When doing so, it's essential to understand one key point:
The spiciness of Real wasabi comes from volatile compounds that quickly dissipate when exposed to heat.

Point 1 To Preserve the Spiciness, Avoid Heat

The defining trait of Real wasabi is its delicate, aromatic heat. This spiciness is caused by volatile compounds that are easily lost when heated. If you want to fully enjoy the sharp kick of Real wasabi, add it after cooking, not before. On the flip side, if you prefer a milder flavor, adding it before heating will cause the spiciness to evaporate, leaving behind a gentle aroma. Even with light cooking, the wasabi's healthful properties remain intact.

Point 2 Mixing with Oil Makes Real wasabi Milder

When mixed with oil, the spicy compounds in Real wasabi become coated and mellow in flavor. That's why it pairs so well with fatty ingredients like grilled steak or fatty tuna sashimi—the wasabi balances the richness while enhancing the *umami*. Additionally, coating freshly grated Real wasabi in oil helps preserve its flavor, making it a smart technique for longer-lasting taste and aroma. Incorporating this into your cooking is a delicious and refined way to make the most of Real wasabi.

Part 3

Learn about wasabi

Want to Know More about Wasabi?

There's a surprising amount you may not know about wasabi, from its origins and varieties to how it's cultivated and processed. Discovering more about wasabi will help you enjoy it on a whole new level.

There are all kinds of stories behind the Real wasabi and wasabi products we enjoy today!

Types of Wasabi: What's the Difference?

The classic Japanese Real wasabi

Wasabi can be divided into two major types: Real wasabi (Japanese wasabi) and horseradish. While both belong to the Brassicaceae family, they differ in species, aroma, spiciness, and cultivation methods.

The star of this guide, Real wasabi, is a perennial plant native to Japan. Even within Real wasabi, there are two main varieties: *sawa*-wasabi, grown in mountain streams or spring water, and *hata*-wasabi, cultivated in cool, moist fields. Most Japanese people associate wasabi with the stream-grown *sawa*-wasabi, which thrives in clean, abundant water at temperatures between 8–18°C (46–64°F). This makes it a specialty crop grown in limited regions such as Shizuoka, Nagano, and Shimane Prefectures. Grated Real wasabi is a pale green paste with a slightly sticky texture, a pungent spiciness that hits the nose, and a fresh, grassy aroma.

The wasabi most people actually eat is horseradish

Horseradish is a perennial plant native to Europe, introduced to Japan in the late 1800s. It's com-

WASABI DATA

Real wasabi
(Eutrema japonicum)

Pungent Compound

Allyl isothiocyanate (volatile)

Key Characteristics

- Refreshing, clean aroma
- Bright green color
- Slight stickiness when freshly grated

Main Production

Japan (Shizuoka, Nagano, Iwate, Shimane)

WASABI DATA

Horseradish
(Armoracia rusticana)

Pungent Compound

Allyl isothiocyanate (volatile)

Key Characteristics

- Sharp, intense spiciness
- Coarse, fibrous texture
- Bright white color when grated

Main Production

Northern Europe, North America, China, and Japan (Hokkaido)

monly served with roast beef or used in sauces. Hardy and fast-growing, horseradish has thick roots and can be found growing wild in places like Hokkaido, where it's affectionately known as *yama*-wasabi (mountain wasabi). In Hokkaido households, it's often grated and served over hot rice—a comforting local flavor. Grated horseradish is white, has little stickiness, and offers a sharper, more radish-like flavor compared to Real wasabi. Due to its high yield and lower cost, horseradish is widely used as the main ingredient in powdered wasabi and shelf-stable wasabi tubes. That means the "wasabi" most people are used to eating is, in fact, not Real wasabi, but horseradish.

WASABI COLUMN

Used in Processed Wasabi

Compared to Real wasabi, horseradish is hardier, has thicker roots, and yields higher harvests. It's easier to grow and thus frequently used as the main ingredient in commercial wasabi products, such as shelf-stable wasabi paste in tubes. You can often confirm this by checking the ingredients label—horseradish is clearly listed.

A Long History with the Japanese People

Wasabi as a traditional medicinal plant

Though wasabi is now a familiar condiment in Japanese cuisine, its use dates back to ancient times, where it was appreciated for its medicinal properties.

Archaeological findings at the Asuka Palace Garden site in Asuka Village, Nara Prefecture, uncovered wooden tablets listing plant names believed to include wasabi and other herbs, along with references to administrative offices in charge of garden management. This suggests that wasabi was recognized and utilized as early as the Asuka Period (538–710 CE).

In the Heian Period (794–1185), wasabi appears in Japan's oldest medical herb encyclopedia *Honzo Wamyo* under the name "wasabi." It is also listed in the *Engishiki*, a 10th-century collection of laws and customs, as "wasabi"—notably recorded as a tax tribute collected from regions near Kyoto, including Wakasa, Echizen, Tango, Tajima, and Inaba.

Wasabi cultivation is believed to have begun in the early Edo Period (1603–1868), specifically during the Keicho era (1596–1615), in Utougi in the upper reaches of the Abe River, Shizuoka City. It was around this time that *nigiri-zushi* with wasabi was first created, igniting a culinary trend in Edo (modern-day Tokyo) and spreading wasabi's popularity among the common people. Back then, without refrigeration, people learned through experience that wasabi helped suppress fishy odors and prevent foodborne illnesses. It was a natural antibacterial agent that became an essential part of Japan's food culture.

Asuka Period

600

Mention of wasabi on wooden tablet excavated from the Asuka Capital Site

The Archaeological Institute of Kashihara in Nara Prefecture, which analyzed wooden tablets unearthed in Asuka Village, Nara, announced: "The tablets were approximately 8 to 30 cm in length and featured names of plants that may be referring to wasabi and other medicinal herbs, as well as the names of government offices responsible for managing gardens."

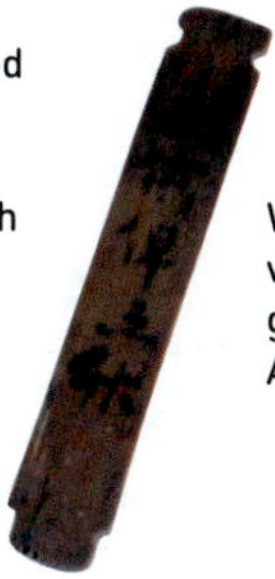

Wooden tablet excavated from an herbal garden from the Asuka period

Heian Period

800

Mention of "wasabi" in Japan's oldest herb encyclopedia

Japan's oldest medical herb encyclopedia, *Honzo Wamyo*, contains a reference to "wasabi," suggesting that wasabi has long been used as a medicinal herb.

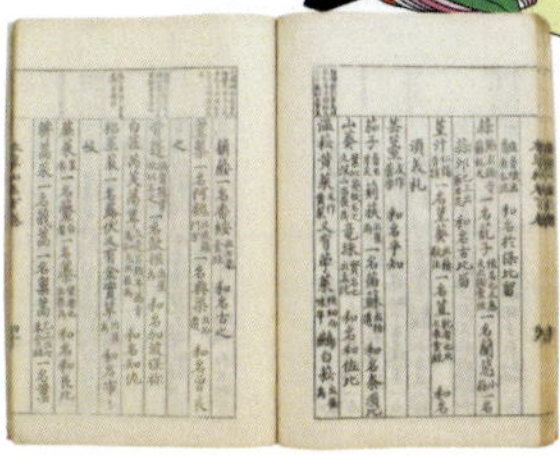

Japan's oldest medicinal herb encyclopedia, *Honzo Wamyo*

Kamakura Period

1200

Mention of "wasabi" in Kamakura-era (1185–1333) cookbook

It is believed that wasabi was consumed in a cold soup called *hiyajiru*. Wasabi is mentioned in *Chujiruiki*, a cookbook from the Kamakura period. In the section describing offerings of *hiyajiru*, it says: "For the ingredients of the soup: add wasabi, summer knotweed.
Leaves, salt, grated yam, and *tachibana* citrus leaves, and serve them all together on one plate."

Muromachi Period

Mention of "wasabi" in a *terakoya* (temple school) textbook and family cookbook

In the *terakoya* (temple school) textbook *Teikin Orai*, wasabi is mentioned alongside *hiyajiru* cold soup, suggesting that it was eaten as part of meals served at Buddhist services. In the *Shijoryu Hochosho*, a family cookbook from the 1400s, there is a note that says: "For carp: wasabi vinegar."

1400

Azuchi-Momoyama Period

Mention of dishes using wasabi in cookbook

In the cookbook *Kokin Chomishu*, wasabi appears as an ingredient in various dishes such as *isona-tamago* eggs, plum kernel eggs, Ise tofu, and red fish cake.(*from Wasabi no nihonshi* [Japanese history of wasabi] by Yamane Kyoko, Bun-ichi Co., Ltd.)

1600

Edo Period

Tokugawa Ieyasu's affinity for wasabi, the start of cultivation and the *nigiri-zushi* boom

Tokugawa clan's holly-hock crest

Tokugawa Ieyasu, the founder and first shogun of the Tokugawa shogunate,was known both as a gourmet and a health enthusiast. He was presented with wasabi and became extremely fond of its flavor. It is said that because wasabi leaves resembled the Tokugawa clan's hollyhock crest, it was declared a secret not to be taken outside the clan. In the Edo period (1603–1868), wasabi was eaten with sashimi, vinegared fish and vegetables, and soba noodles. In the mid-1800s, *nigiri-zushi* became popular, and with wasabi being used, it spread rapidly.

1900

Taisho Period

Konagaya Yoshichi invents powdered wasabi

The development of powdered wasabi—the origin of processed wasabi—dates to the early 1900s. Shizuoka-based tea broker Konagaya Yoshichi came up with the idea of drying raw wasabi like tea, powdering it, and selling it. It became quite popular at restaurants and inns, leading him to begin full-scale production in 1920, marking the start of mass production.

Showa Period

Paste wasabi
(for food service use) 1971

Shelf-stable tube wasabi
(for home use) 1972

Freshly grated wasabi, raw grated wasabi 1973

In 1973, the now-standard raw grated wasabi made from Real wasabi was developed.by kinjirushi Co., Ltd.

As product lines expanded, health and beauty benefits derived from wasabi—such as antioxidants, detoxification, improved blood circulation, and improved skin—drew attention, leading to the development of health foods and cosmetics.

Heisei Period

Wasabi-based supplements 2004

Wasabi-based cosmetics 2005

A wide variety of wasabi products, health foods to cosmetics

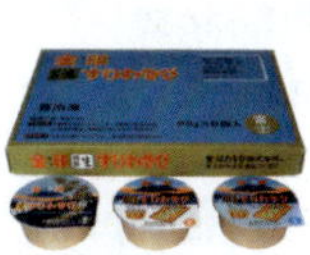

Kinjirushi flesh grated wasabi

Kinjirushi powdered wasabi

Kinjirushi grated wasabi

Kinjirushi wasabi paste

Reiwa Period

Approved as a functional food with the claim "Reported to support aspects of cognitive function, such as judgment (the ability to accurately process information) **and attention, in middle-aged and elderly individuals without regular exercise habits."** 2019

2021—Wasabi-Sulfinyl™ Receives U.S. FDA Self-GRAS Certification
(Self-GRAS is a required self-submission system for selling functional ingredients in the U.S.) 2021

Approved as a functional food with the claim "Reported to improve memory in elderly people." 2025

2000

The Difference Between Shelf-Stable Tube Wasabi and Real wasabi

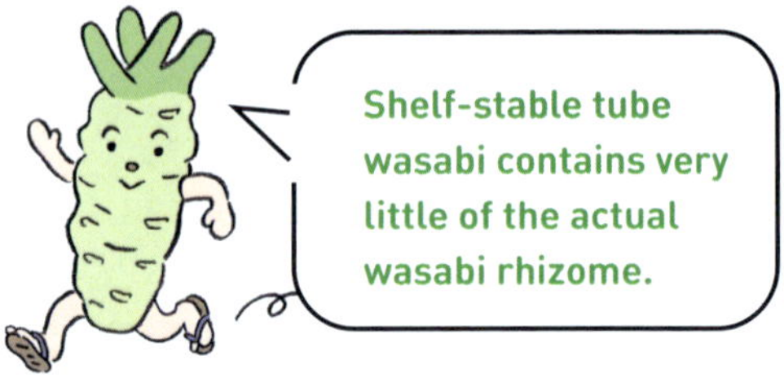

Features of Real wasabi and wasabi products

Real wasabi's beneficial compound, hexaraphane, is largely absent from shelf-stable tube wasabi. Even products labeled as using Real wasabi often contain mainly the stem portion, rather than the rhizome where hexaraphane is most concentrated.

Shelf-stable wasabi paste is also characterized by the inclusion of various additives, such as salt, starch, oils, and thickeners, used to enhance its shelf life. As a result, its taste is noticeably different from that of Real wasabi.

Shelf-stable tube wasabi contains almost no health benefits.

In contrast, frozen or refrigerated wasabi products are processed in a way that helps retain the natural aroma and pungency of fresh wasabi, and they tend to contain fewer additives. If you have the opportunity, try comparing Real wasabi to your usual tube wasabi. You'll likely notice that the tube version has a much stronger, saltier kick, whereas Real wasabi offers a more refined sharpness and a clean, refreshing flavor. That said, the convenience and affordability of shelf-stable wasabi make it hard to part with. The important thing is to understand the characteristics of each and use them appropriately depending on the dish and the occasion.

Characteristics of Shelf Stable Tube Wasabi

Price	Low
Shelf life	Long
Ingredients	Contains many ingredients other than wasabi (salt, starch, oil, thickening agents, horseradish, wasabi stem etc.)
Taste	Quite spicy and salty
Health benefits	Almost none

Characteristics of Real wasabi

Price	High
Shelf life	Short
Ingredients	Rhizome of Real wasabi (100%)
Taste	Refreshing aroma and flavor, moderate spiciness
Health benefits	Hexapharane

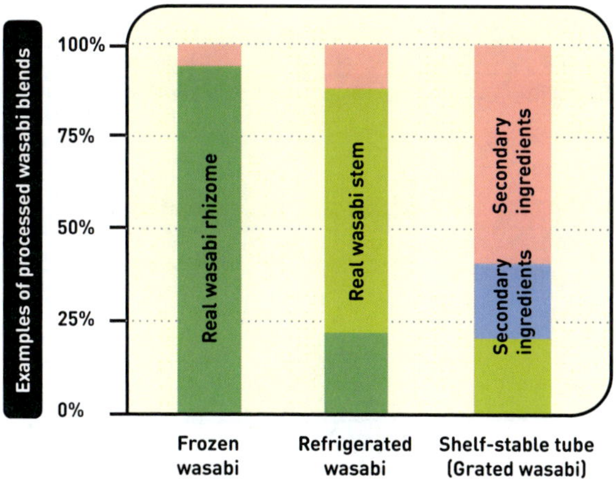

Shelf-stable wasabi in tubes contains a lot of secondary ingredients to improve its shelf life!

*This graph is an example. The actual ingredients vary by product. Some room temperature wasabi tubes do not contain horseradish.

The Science Behind the Flavors of Real wasabi

The spiciness and aroma first arise when wasabi is grated!

The pungency and aroma of Real wasabi are born from enzymatic reactions

To fully enjoy the flavor of Real wasabi, it helps to understand the science behind its deliciousness. Let's take a closer look at the two elements at the heart of Real wasabi's appeal: its pungency and aroma. Interestingly, Real wasabi isn't spicy when licked or bitten into directly.

That pungency and aroma are only created when it is grated. This is because the grating process destroys the plant's cells and triggers an enzymatic reaction. The pungency peaks about 3 to 5 minutes after grating, and then gradually evaporates until it fades away completely.

Finely grating the wasabi draws out more of its pungent compounds, so it's best to use a specially designed fine-grater for the job.

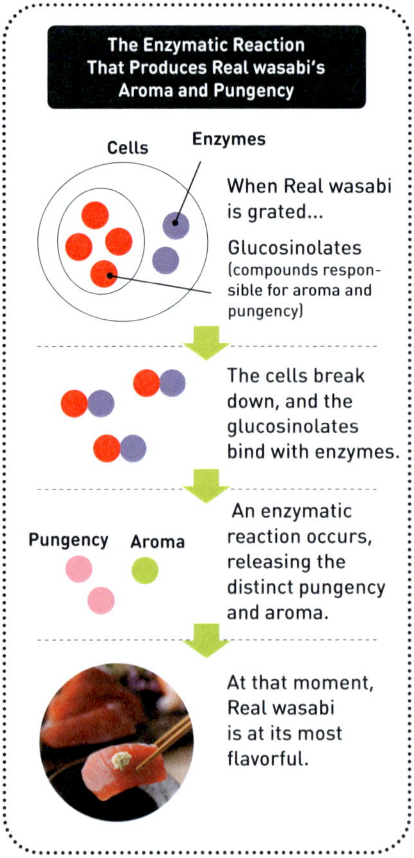

Pungency and Aroma Compounds in Real wasabi and Horseradish

*Major Isothiocyanates (ITC)

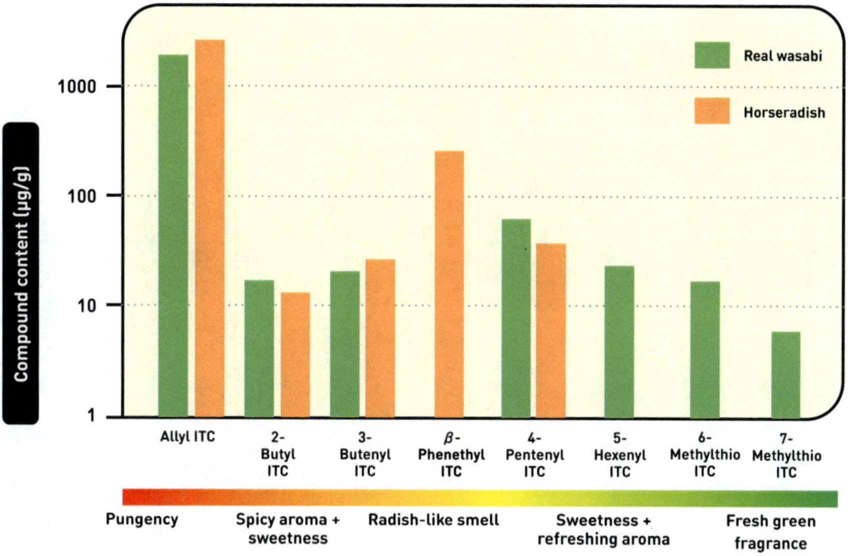

An analysis of Real wasabi revealed that it contains more than ten different types of aroma compounds. While horseradish has a distinctive radish-like smell, the refreshing and clean scent of Real wasabi is due to differences in its chemical makeup.

Duration of Pungency and Aroma

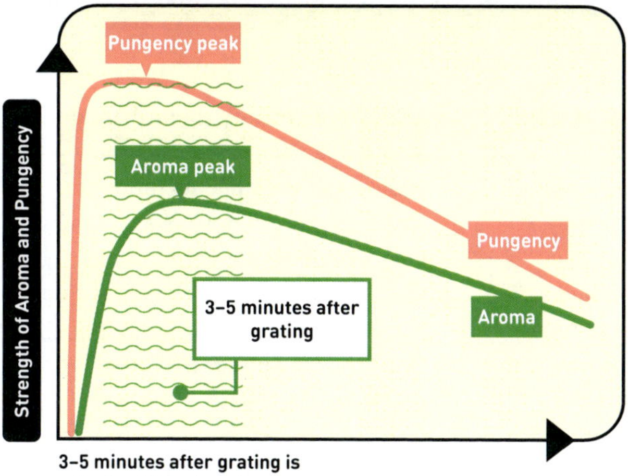

3–5 minutes after grating is the best time to enjoy it.

Real wasabi and horseradish have the same pungency components, but there is a big difference in their aromatic components!

After Real wasabi is grated, its aroma and pungency peak within 3 to 5 minutes. Since the pungent compounds are highly volatile, they quickly dissipate thereafter. Remember: Real wasabi is at its most flavorful within about 30 minutes of grating.

How Real wasabi is Grown and Delivered

Ensuring a stable supply of wasabi to Japanese tables

How do Real wasabi and processed wasabi products make their way to our dining tables? While many people have at least a vague idea of how rice is grown, few are familiar with the journey of wasabi.

Wasabi farmers cultivate the plants, then manufacturers process the harvested wasabi into products and distribute them. That may sound like a fairly typical supply chain—but wasabi cultivation is anything but ordinary. Wasabi must be grown in cool environments year-round and requires more than a year to mature. It is highly sensitive to direct sunlight, making it one of the most delicate agricultural products. Its production areas are also limited, with only a few regions

such as Shizuoka, Nagano, Iwate, and Shimane prefectures serving as the primary growing sites.

In recent years, opportunities to enjoy fresh wasabi in Japan have declined, and domestic production is also decreasing. Add to that the effects of climate change and global warming, and the challenges facing the industry only grow more complex. In order to continue delivering this delicate and temperamental ingredient to our tables in a stable manner, collaboration across the entire wasabi industry is essential.

In the following sections, we'll take a closer look at the dedication of wasabi farmers and the initiatives of manufacturers working to sustain this unique ingredient.

A Deep Dive into Real wasabi Production

Time-intensive, rare and all the more delicious

The Nakaizu region of Shizuoka Prefecture is one of Japan's leading production areas for Real wasabi. The pristine, cold water that springs from Mt. Amagi, known as a natural reservoir, creates an ideal environment for cultivating high-quality, flavorful wasabi. We spoke with Joji Asada, who continues to grow wasabi in this exceptional region, to learn more about the craft behind its cultivation.

When asked about the challenges of wasabi farming, Asada explains, "The biggest issue is the weather. Mt. Amagi typically sees 2,000 to 3,000 mm of rainfall annually, but lately, likely due to global warming, we've been seeing more torrential downpours and sudden cloudbursts. When that happens, the mountain, which should act like a natural reservoir, doesn't have time to store the rain.

The water flows straight down, and in the worst cases, it can wash away entire wasabi fields or plants. On top of that, the extreme heat we've seen recently is also a major threat to wasabi.

This year, a lot of our plants have suffered because of it."

"Compared to the past, wasabi is becoming much harder to grow," Asada continues. He points out that Japan's declining wasabi production is not only due to climate change but also wildlife damage from animals

Asada's wasabi is characterized by its stickiness. When grated, the rhizome sticks to the grater. The photo on the right shows wasabi fields covered with shade cloths.

Joji Asada

The Asada family has been farming wasabi in Izu for generations, and Joji Asada's wasabi has won numerous awards, including the Minister of Agriculture, Forestry and Fisheries Award and the Forestry Agency Director-General Award.

It takes a year and a half for wasabi to be ready for shipment, but that's what makes it so delicious!

Asada harvesting wasabi, which he has cultivated with love. He feels that climate change has made wasabi cultivation more difficult than in the past.

like deer and wild boar. As these pressures increase, more wasabi farmers are being forced to abandon the work.

Time-intensive, rare and all the more delicious

Wasabi is an incredibly delicate plant that can't grow unless the environmental conditions are just right. In Nakaizu, the wasabi fields spread across terraced landscapes built using the *tatami-ishi* method—a traditional technique where the ground is excavated, then layered with large stones, medium stones, and finally fine gravel and sand. This functions as a natural filtration system, allowing clean water to flow continuously from one terraced field to the next.

This ingenious cultivation method creates optimal conditions for wasabi to thrive.

Carefully Grown Wasabi—Tightly Packed and Full of Flavor

Providing clean water alone isn't enough to satisfy wasabi. Maintaining a stable water temperature throughout the year is also critical—10 to 15°C is considered ideal. Since wasabi is also sensitive to direct sunlight, shade cloths are essential for protecting the plants. Farmers must also be vigilant against damage from wild animals, such as wild boars.

There are many factors to monitor constantly, which makes wasabi cultivation particularly demanding. And because it is grown on sloped terrain, the work is difficult to mechanize—another reason why Real wasabi is so rare and valuable.

Passing wasabi cultivation to the next generation

When we asked Asada what he considers most important in cultivating wasabi, he answered without hesitation: "Love. That's what it all comes down to. Showing love means taking the time to do small things—like shutting off the water during a typhoon or shielding the plants when the sun is too strong. It's about tending to every little need. Honestly, I'm always checking the weather forecast. I've even gone out in the middle of the night with a flashlight to check on the fields."

Asada also emphasized that choosing the right variety of wasabi is crucial to cultivating flavorful plants. "You have to understand the specific conditions of the stream you manage, and plant a variety that suits it. Otherwise, it just won't work."

Although wasabi can technically

The photo on the left shows letters of appreciation and essays sent by elementary school children who participated in the Real wasabi experience. The children were fascinated seeing Real wasabi for the first time, as shown in the photo on the right.

be harvested year-round, it takes about 18 months for the plants to reach shipping size. And because there's no way to know whether a variety will thrive in a given stream without trying it, the early stages of cultivation often involve trial and error. Once a harvest is complete, new seedlings are planted right away to begin the cycle again.

"We send our carefully selected wasabi and seeds to Kinjirushi, where they help us grow strong seedlings, either from seed or through a process called mericlone*," explains Asada.

"If we had to grow seedlings ourselves, it would be just too much work and too risky." He says his greatest joy is when a batch of wasabi comes out exactly as he envisioned.

Asada is also actively involved in promoting wasabi cultivation. He mentors young people interested in farming, and teaches local elementary school students about wasabi. The children, amazed at seeing Real wasabi for the first time, often write essays about the experience. Asada keeps many of them. "I just want kids to know what Real wasabi is from a young age," he says with a smile.

*A method in which the growth tip of a plant is removed and grown in a sterile medium.

Delivering Essential Wasabi Seedlings across Japan

At Kinjirushi's agri-business research center, ongoing efforts are dedicated to developing wasabi that is robust, flavorful, and rich in health-beneficial compounds.

Their earliest work began with regenerating disease-free seedlings of horseradish from its apical meristems—the growth tips at the ends of roots and stems, where viruses cannot penetrate.

Countless test tubes containing cultivated wasabi are lined up at Kinjirushi Agri Co., Ltd. Agricultural Products Division. Factors including temperature and lighting are meticulously controlled, and the resulting high-quality seedlings are delivered to farmers.

By extracting this tiny portion under a microscope and growing it in test tubes, researchers could regenerate healthy, virus-free plants.

They also developed disease-resistant varieties by cross-breeding strong parent plants, and even induced horseradish, which rarely produces seeds, to generate them. Each seedling was raised and studied individually to identify favorable traits. From this work, a disease-resistant variety was born and introduced into cultivation in 2004, dramatically increasing the yield of wasabi used in processing.

Today, the technologies honed through horseradish cultivation are being applied to Real wasabi seedling development. There's a saying in agriculture: "Success is halfway there if you have good seedlings." This applies perfectly to Real wasabi. Stable access to high-quality seedlings is absolutely essential for wasabi farmers.

The part of the plant where viruses cannot penetrate, called the apical meristems, is cut off and cultivated. By dividing the cultivated wasabi seedlings, it is possible to mass-produce high quality copies.

The Kinjirushi agribusiness research center conducts research on various plants in addition to wasabi and horseradish.

Wasabi grown in test tubes thrives in wasabi production areas across Japan

Smaller seedlings are better for transporting upstream to the wasabi fields. Smaller seedlings that fare just as well as larger ones have been successfully developed.

A stable supply of high-quality seedlings supports the wasabi industry!

However, there is a chronic shortage of Real wasabi seedlings in Japan. One major factor is the aging of seedling producers. This shortage threatens to weaken wasabi-growing regions and is a serious concern for everyone involved in the industry.

That's why the development of superior Real wasabi varieties and reliable seedling supply is now seen as a central mission for the wasabi industry.

As a wasabi processing company, Kinjirushi is also committed to sourcing the best raw ingredients. This includes not only flavor and vigor, but also ensuring that the wasabi contains high levels of health-promoting compounds, such as hexaraphane.

Afterword

Thank you for reading this book all the way through.

If this book has helped shift your perception of Real wasabi even slightly, compared to before you picked it up, then I consider its purpose fulfilled.

Japanese people have been using Real wasabi since ancient times. Yet in recent years, convenience and cost have come to overshadow flavor and health benefits, leaving the true essence of Real wasabi less appreciated. Even so, we're beginning to see a renewed spotlight on wasabi. The global boom in Japanese cuisine has sparked fresh interest overseas, and scientific research continues to uncover new health-promoting properties of this unique plant.

In today's aging society, where lifespans are extending beyond 100 years, there's growing focus not only on physical health but also on brain health. The cognitive benefits of Real wasabi are something we believe deserve widespread attention moving forward. Alzheimer's and other forms of dementia are conditions for which no definitive cure exists, but Real wasabi may offer a ray of hope.

This book has explored why Real wasabi has such potential, focusing particularly on a beneficial compound found in its rhizome called hexaraphane. We also introduced the idea of incorporating wasabi into daily life—what we call Wasabi Wellness—and shared various recipe ideas to make it both enjoyable and delicious.

Of course, starting and maintaining any new health habit is not always easy. But with a Wasabi Wellness routine, the barrier to entry is refreshingly low, and it's tasty, too. Just a teaspoon a day is enough. And if you're pressed for time, supplements are a good alternative.

I sincerely hope that this book encourages you to bring a little more wasabi into your daily life. It would be wonderful if that new habit contributes even a little to your well-being.

Lastly, I'd like to express my deepest gratitude to Kinjirushi Co., Ltd., whose unwavering support and understanding made this research possible. In particular, I owe a special thanks to Chairman Ikko Kobayashi and Vice Chairman Keiko Kobayashi, who have supported me patiently for over 20 years.

I also extend heartfelt thanks to the many university professors and farmers, both in Japan and abroad, who offered guidance and cooperation. And I'm especially grateful to the dedicated researchers and staff within our own company. It is thanks to all of you that we've gradually been able to shed light on the health benefits of wasabi and, ultimately, achieve the results presented here on its cognitive-enhancing potential.

With deep appreciation,
Isao Okunishi, Ph.D.
(Agricultural Science)
Kinjirushi Co., Ltd.

Staff
Design: Midori Kondo
Illustration: Reina Yamanaka
Photography: Jun Matsuki (SHUFUNOTOMO Co., Ltd.)
Proofreading: Tokyo Shuppan Service Center
Production Management: Yohei Nakayama (FORWAY Co., Ltd.)
Production: Taku Kazama
Editor: Toru Nakagawa (Shufunotomo Co., Ltd.)

Medical Supervision: Takakazu Oka
Professor and Chair of Psychosomatic Medicine, School of Medicine, International University of Health and Welfare. His specialties include the treatment of psychogenic fever, chronic fatigue syndrome, orthostatic dysregulation, and functional gastrointestinal disorders.